RIVERS DELIVERS

RIVERS DELIVERS

MARION RIVERS RAVENEL

WYRICK & COMPANY

Published by Wyrick & Company
P.O. Box 89
Charleston, SC 29402

Designed by Sally Heineman
Manufactured in the United States of America.

Library of Congress Cataloging-in-Publication-Data

Ravenel, Marion Rivers, 1943-
Rivers delivers / by Marion Rivers Ravenel
p. cm.
Includes bibliographical references and index.
ISBN 0-941711-24-2 : $19.95
1. Rivers, L. Mendel (Lucius Mendel), 1905-1970. 2. Legislators—
United States—Biography. 3. United States. Congress. House—
Biography. I. Title.
E748.R47R38 1994
328.73'092—dc20   94-94-30240

CIP

The following publishers have generously given permission to use quotations from copyrighted works: From *The Best and the Brightest*, by David Halberstam. Copyright 1969, 1971, 1972 by David Halberstam. Reprinted by permission of Random House. From *Inside the House* by Daniel Rapoport. Copyright 1975 by Daniel Rapoport. Reprinted by permission of Esquire, Inc. From *The Drew Pearson Story* by Frank Kluckhorn and Jay Franklin. Copyright 1967 by Frank Kluckhorn. Reprinted by permission of Hallberg Publishing Corp. From *The Pied Piper: Allard Lowenstein and the Liberal Dream* by Richard Cummings. Copyright 1985 by Richard Cummings. Reprinted by permission of Grove Press, Inc. From *Fishbait—The Memoirs of the Congressional Doorkeeper* by William "Fishbait" Miller, as told to Frances Spatz Leighton. Copyright 1977. From "Can a Congressman sue a columnist?", by Donald R. Shanor, *Columbia Journalism Review*, Spring 1967. Reprinted by permission of Columbia Journalism Review. From "The Washington Merry-Go-Round" by Drew Pearson. Reprinted by permission of United Feature Syndicate Inc./United Media.

With love, to the memory of my father

PREFACE

This is a book about my father.

When I first sat down, several years ago, to begin this book, I realized almost immediately that it would be one of the hardest things I had ever attempted.

How in the world was I ever going to put him into words? How was I going to describe someone who, for most of my life, I had found difficult to even talk to? I honestly thought the undertaking would become easier as I got into it. It didn't.

He was to me a great many things—demanding, caring, unyielding, impatient, loving and unpredictable. But he was *not* going to be easy to describe.

He was the best and worst of fathers...just like probably every other father in history.

Like many children of public figures, I had a hard time finding a niche where I felt I belonged in his life. He was, to be honest, oftentimes a far better public person than he was a private one. But he was there for me when I needed him.

My father went to Congress before I was born, and he died, in office, when I was in my mid-20s. His years in public office spanned some of the most dramatic in America's history. This country was in the depths of the Great Depression when he was first elected in 1940, and quickly moved into involvement in a global war that seemed to turn everything and everybody upside down. Following that, a "Cold War" threatened the world with fears of nuclear explosions, coupled with years of unprecedented domestic prosperity. For more than a decade of my father's last years in Congress, violence in our country horrified Americans, only to be compounded by participation in an Asian war that influenced and divided the feelings of Americans more profoundly than may ever be realized.

It surprises me to this day what a sheltered life I led, politically speaking, growing up. For the most part, my father did not expose his family to the frequently harsh and cruel glare of the political spotlight— a spotlight that he enjoyed thoroughly. My mother has frequently admitted that she went into the political world with him kicking and screaming. For all the public adulation and applause that a prominent political figure might receive, it can make for some fairly lonely families in the background.

I was 22 years old before I ever entertained more than a cursory examination of the views of my father. He had just become the Chairman of the House Armed Services Committee, and all hell had broken loose over the Vietnam War. Suddenly, he was a popular subject for out-and-out hero worship from his supporters, and a target for stinging, mocking criticism from his critics.

When I moved to San Francisco in 1966, and my father had been Chairman for about 18 months, I was totally unprepared for the prominence that he had on a national level. It was a little frightening for me.

I am aware of the fact that, as his daughter, I have certain unique qualifications to write about him. Then again, I may, perhaps, be totally unsuited to attempt a biographical sketch of him. I am the first to admit that I, quite naturally, harbor untold subjective prejudices about him, but I trust that the readers will recognize that I have tried to be as honest and candid as I can.

There are many images of my father that often come to mind. Like the time in southern Germany in 1969 when he drove me down the autobahn from Frankfurt in my brand new car. Here we were, an obviously older man with white, fairly long, hair blowing in the wind beside a young woman many years his junior going a million miles an hours in a sports car, no less. For all the other people seeing us fly past, if they cared to think about it, here was one of those couples that might be ridiculed. It is one of my favorite memories.

Or the time that I, a newly-licensed driver, confidently drove into the garage in my mother's car as she and my father watched. I died a thousand deaths as I heard the unmistakable sounds of my "expertise" as the chrome strip was peeled away when I scraped the side of the entrance. Certain to be cussed out for my "stupidity," I broke into sobs, but my father laughed instead and gave me a hug, advising me to be more careful the next time.

But there is one single incident that has remained with me in perfect perspective, and that in many ways speaks volumes about him:

On a chilly autumn afternoon in 1960, Daddy's black Chrysler pulled into the driveway of our home in Alexandria, Virginia. I had been expecting his arrival for some time. Although tired from the long, ten-hour drive up from Charleston, he emerged from the car with a smile, pulling his favorite red tartan Tam o' Shanter onto his head. He quickly greeted me with a hug and we prepared to unload the car.

Suddenly, the automobile began to roll down the driveway, a steep, downward-sloping grade by the hillside house. In horror, I watched the runaway machine as it began to move, gaining speed, veering slightly to one side. I remember feeling completely paralyzed.

But my father, without a moment's hesitation, bolted after it, yanked open the driver's door and brought it to a halt just split seconds before it would have headed over an embankment. That he could have been crushed by the car apparently never entered his mind.

"The goddamned emergency brake must have slipped off," he softly commented as he emerged, completely unruffled, from the car.

This was the father that I remember: quick to act, absolutely fearless, generally making the right decision, and, knowing that, going on with things.

It has been nearly a quarter of a century since the death of my father. The one thing that has never ceased to amaze me is the way people who knew my father are so anxious to tell me a story about him. For a long time, I thought people were just being polite. But it's more than that.

Out of the blue, someone tells me of his experience as an Army officer in Panama when he was unable to cut through the red tape to get furniture for his quarters. Only when the sergeant in charge learned that he was from Mendel Rivers' home district did he seem even slightly interested in paying attention to the officer's request. And, then, he gave the officer everything he had wanted, and then some.

Several people have recounted in great detail the problems they and their families experienced in trying to bring a soldier or sailor home to the bedside of a dying parent. The young person was home almost immediately once my father had learned of the issue. And these were not necessarily voting constituents, either.

More than 20 years after the experience, a publisher told me that he and his 12 year old son were among a group of people walking down a hall in the Capitol with my father as he and other Congressmen were discussing the military budget. Suddenly, in a mid-sentence reference to the billions involved in the budget, my father stopped at a concession counter and called back to the publisher's son and said: "Son, what kind of candy bar do you want?" Seconds after purchasing the candy, the conversation resumed about the billions of dollars.

Recently, there was a letter to the editor published in the Charleston *Post and Courier* which, nearly a quarter of a century after my father's death, stated "I had known Mendel Rivers (and I wasn't even a native South Carolinian), as being more admired by those in the military than any living human in the world. He was popular, respected, hard working and effective. There has to be more like him."

He undoubtedly did things throughout his life that displeased many people, but the stories that I am constantly told are about how he used the powers of his position to help others, not himself. For me, these are the things that made his life very worthwhile.

I hope that I have been able to present a reasonable portrait of him. He would expect no less from me.

I could never have done this book without the assistance of my mother who gave me not only information but, more importantly, encouragement. Thank you, with much love.

And to the many, many people who have helped me in countless ways, I extend my sincere thanks, especially: my sister, Peg Eastman; my brother, Mendel Rivers, Jr.; my aunt, Dorothy Anderson; Coralee Bull; Joe Riley, Sr.; Tom Waring; Elsa McDowell; Nan Morrison; Anne de la Morandiore; Sally Lee; Arthur Rashap; Clark Hobbie; Frank Jameson; Russ Blandford; Ted Stern; Mendel J. Davis; Palmer Gaillard, Jr.; Tony Harrigan; William Humphreys; and Leon Banov, Jr.

Marion Rivers Ravenel

RIVERS DELIVERS

CHAPTER 1

"You know, I told you I am a country boy. I don't know about national politics," L. Mendel Rivers concluded in his interview on NBC's *Meet the Press* in April of 1967. I watched the program that day with a friend in San Francisco, where I was living at the time. It seemed so corny and provincial for my father to be saying that on national television to a panel of seemingly worldly, sophisticated and urbane journalists. Yet he delivered the statement with a twinkle in his eye.

He had held his own in front of the serious, inquiring journalists as they jumped from topic to topic-everything from draft dodgers to civil rights to controversies regarding the conduct of the war in Vietnam. They had not been hostile, but not exactly sympathetic, either.

It was a long time later when I realized that my father used references to his rural upbringing effectively to disarm an unsuspecting audience. And, by the time of the airing of this particular interview, he, in fact, knew a great deal about national politics.

He took great pleasure throughout his life in volunteering that he was "just a country boy from Gumville in Hell Hole Swamp." This was, in fact, accurate, but his origins were not quite as humble as he made them sound.

My grandfather, Lucius Hampton Rivers, was born in 1864 in Sumter, South Carolina, and was orphaned at an early age. He grew up in nearby St. George with the family of his aunt, Lula Mims, whose husband, Iverson, adopted him. From a young age, Lucius worked with his uncle in the lumber and turpentine business, a thriving industry in the South in the late 1800s. By the time he was in his early 30s, he was in business for himself near St. Stephen, in Berkeley County, some 50 miles north of Charleston.

From the moment he met Henrietta Marion McCay in 1895, Lucius determined that he would marry her. "Etta" was the favorite daughter of Thomas A. McCay, the prosperous owner of Sugarloaf Plantation. She was, however, engaged at the time to a man from the town of Camden, and the match had the blessing of the McCay family as one which would assure a suitable future for their daughter. The McCays were proud people, and particularly proud of the large land holdings that they had amassed. My great-grandmother counted among her notable forebears Gabriel Marion, brother of the Revolutionary War hero, Francis Marion, "the Swamp Fox."

Thomas McCay had high hopes for his pretty fair-haired daughter. She was among the privileged few women of that era who attended college, studying in the upper part of the state at Greenville College for Women shortly after it opened in 1894.

When Lucius' courtship of his daughter proved to be serious, Mr. McCay forbade her to see the young man. But the couple was not to be dissuaded. One evening in 1896, Lucius backed a wagon up to a window of her father's home and helped Etta to climb out. Their elopement so enraged her father that he promptly disowned her.

To my knowledge, my grandmother never reconciled with her father. Long after her death, I read a letter that she had received from her father shortly after her marriage. Sadly, it was a scathing attack upon her and her new husband.

Spurred, no doubt, by his in-laws' disapproval of his marriage to their daughter, Lucius continued to prove himself. It must have galled the McCays to see just how well he succeeded.

The couple began their married life in a simple but sturdy frame house that Lucius built in the country. Their first child, Earle, was born in 1897. My grandfather worked hard, buying up timber land for his lumber and turpentine business, and farm acreage on which his tenant farmers cultivated cotton. As his business grew, so did his family.

Berniece was born in 1899, Blanche in 1901, and Mildred in 1903.

Late in September, 1905, my grandmother gave birth to her fifth child, whom she named Lucius Mendel.

The Jewish name of Mendel was explained many years later when my father responded to an inquiry about it from the editor of a Jewish newspaper: "I am quite well aware of the fact that Mendel is one of the oldest Jewish names and I have received many compliments on having been selected to bear it. I was named for one of the great lawyers of South Carolina—the late Mendel L. Smith of Camden, to whom, at one time, my mother was engaged. He was a great orator and a great public servant. I try to follow in his footsteps to the hilt of my limited capacity...I have always enjoyed particularly close association with numerous people of the Jewish faith and I believe my name is responsible, to a great extent, for the exceptionally kind feelings they have, at all times, displayed to me."

That my grandmother, obviously with her husband's approval, would name her child for the man to whom she was engaged when she met her future husband is nothing less than amazing to me.

Thomas McCay died about a month after the birth of his grandson Mendel.

The Rivers family moved to a new house on the Bonneau Road near St. Stephen soon after the birth of their sixth child, Marguerite Lebby, in 1907. My grandfather spared little in building the home for his family.

The house must have been very impressive, particularly for the era in which it was built and for its rural location. It is a somewhat commanding Victorian two-story frame structure with eight spacious rooms, a large entrance hall, high ceilings and broad welcoming front porch. The downstairs had a parlor, sitting room, dining room and guest room. Upstairs were the family bedrooms—Daddy shared one with his brother. Rugs covered the heart pine floors, and a porch leading from the dining room to the exterior kitchen house which held the ice box. Beyond the kitchen was the acetylene building which housed the generator for the gas light fixtures in all of the rooms.

The house was surrounded by nearly 600 acres of land, many of which contained apple and pear orchards bordered by timberland. Three tenant houses were on the property and 15 employees were hired for the various jobs. My grandfather had acquired the property for around $2 an acre, but it was heavily mortgaged.

By local standards, though, the Rivers family was regarded as well situated in an area that was still struggling with the economic ravages of the Reconstruction era following the Civil War.

A successful farmer, my grandfather also owned a sawmill, a cotton gin and a general store, and served as a county superintendent of highways. A great source of pride to the family was that he was the second person in Berkeley County to own an automobile, a Ford, complete with a Klaxon horn.

Visitors in the home frequently stayed for weeks at a time in those days of poor roads and the infancy of the automobile age. A frequent guest was Palmer Gaillard, a land surveyor from Charleston; it was his son who participated in my father's first Congressional campaign and later served for many years as the mayor of Charleston. Aunt Blanche recalled that a Mr. Bimer from Philadelphia, a friend of Theodore Roosevelt, frequently visited when in the vicinity to hunt game on neighboring plantations.

Life for the Rivers children was undoubtedly pleasant in those days. Although the parents were strict disciplinarians, they were also affectionate and generous. Both children and adults of neighboring families were frequently invited for the Rivers' hospitality, and their home became a popular place to visit. A hay wagon was often sent into St. Stephen to pick up a group of children to come out to the house for "candy pulling" and other activities. In the summer months, my grandfather cooled watermelons in sacks that he secured to stumps by the swimming pond he had had built near the house.

Piano lessons were encouraged for the children until the piano teacher's husband arrived inebriated at the house one afternoon. After that, the lessons were abandoned and a player piano was purchased.

Aunt Blanche remembered that the children were always stylishly dressed. Their parents enjoyed bringing back the latest fashions for them on their frequent visits to Charleston. She recalled that at one time she had 27 dresses along with the latest in tassel-trimmed shoes.

My grandmother was apparently both courageous and resourceful. On one occasion when Earle cut his ear severely, she laid him on a trunk and sutured the ear with her sewing needle and thread. "I couldn't have done it better myself," announced their doctor when he examined her stitches.

To accommodate her various skills, she used one of the large upstairs rooms as a workroom where, among other things, she carded wool from their sheep and made several beautifully-constructed mattresses, one for each child. (When my own brother married in 1972, my mother gave him the one which had belonged to my father—it was still in excellent condition after six decades.)

Grandmother helped the local blacks whenever she could. When the members of a black church wanted a fish-shaped weather vane for their steeple, Aunt Blanche told me, my grandmother paid to have it made after she learned that the congregation could not afford it. On many occasions, she helped to bail out black neighbors when jailed on minor infractions.

A loyal and enthusiastic member of the historic St. Stephen Church, my grandmother persuaded her Baptist husband to become an Episcopalian. He, too, became active in the congregation. He financed the restoration of the mid-18th century structure, by having iron bolts installed to repair the damage sustained in the devastating earthquake of 1886 which struck lower South Carolina. All members of the Rivers family have been buried in its churchyard.

The elder Rivers were strict in the observance of the Sabbath. They attended St. Stephen Episcopal Church once a month when the minister, the Reverend Harold Thomas, travelled from the larger town of Florence to conduct the service. On other Sundays they attended one of the other churches in the area, usually Baptist, and sometimes a black church near their home. No one was allowed to play games or participate in other "irreligious" activities on Sundays. Rather, the family gathered in the large parlor where my grandfather read The Story of the Bible to the children every Sunday afternoon. My grandfather read the newspapers there, too, and my father always remembered hearing about the tragic account of the *Titanic* one Sunday in 1912.

In 1910, my grandmother gave birth to twins, William and Jennie. Neither survived for long and my grandmother, ill with blood poisoning, was bedridden for many months. During her convalescence, my grandfather purchased a Shetland pony for the children. "Bessie" delighted them; she was hitched to a wicker cart to take them to school two miles away in St. Stephen. Aunt Blanche told me that one afternoon, hoping to brighten their mother's spirits, the children managed to bring the pony to "visit" my grandmother in the downstairs guest room where she was recuperating.

My grandparents often called my father "Little Man" (an endearment which Daddy later used with his own son). He was a small, thin child, who experienced the expected childhood diseases. Later, it was suggested that he might have been more severely ill as a youngster than recognized. When he was a teenager applying for a job in North Charleston, the examining physician for the obligatory physical exam intimated that he had had rheumatic fever as a child—which would help account for the heart problems he had in later years.

One cold, rainy February afternoon in 1915, my grandfather returned home chilled and feverish, after attending the funeral of a friend. It did not take long for his illness to develop into pneumonia. The country doctor who came to see him recommended brandy to help reduce his chill. The teetotalling patient steadfastly refused.

Blanche was her father's special "pet" as a child. She hated seeing him ill, and stayed way from his sickroom. But one afternoon he sent someone to bring her to him. When she arrived at his bedside, he kept repeating "It will soon be four o'clock...it will soon be four o'clock..." Surrounded by family members and the Reverend Mr. Thomas, my grandfather died as the clock struck four.

He was 51. His nine year old son Mendel stood at the foot of the bed and watched as his father passed away.

For a short time it seemed as though the prosperity of the Rivers family might continue in spite of their tragic loss.

Earle, at the age of 17, was suddenly expected to assume his father's diverse responsibilities. He loved locomotives, not farming. At a very young age, he had learned the whistle of every locomotive that passed through the area. He was a whiz at mechanics and eventually became the Atlantic Coast Line Railroad's top trouble shooter, or wrecking master. Apparently, the title "wrecking master" suited Earle well—he was known to show off when driving automobiles and on several occasions wrecked them in the process.

Earle was still quite young when he married one of the local belles, Alma Jernigan. Aunt Blanche remembered with fondness being in her big brother's wedding as one of several attendants who wore voile dresses with blue lace.

When Earle attempted to manage his in-laws' business interests as well as his own family's, he was disastrously unsuccessful with the latter. My grandmother tried to hold on to the property as best she could. She hired a Mr. Bell to oversee the farm, but it was a poor choice and things got progressively worse.

Several friends, seeing her difficulties, offered to adopt some of her children, but she was determined to keep the family together. The gentleman from Philadelphia, Mr. Bimer, who had been a guest in the home, offered to have Blanche come live with his family. A doctor in Charleston wanted young Mendel to join his family. How different their lives would have been!

When her cousin, the Reverend Robert Lebby, visited the Rivers household, he persuaded my grandmother that the best thing for her to do to save her family was to move and open a boarding house. She took her children from the large farm in the country to a modest six-room frame house on O'Hear Avenue in the small industrial area of North Charleston. It was considered a privileged neighborhood, however, because it was on the trolley car line connecting the community with Charleston and Daddy used to joke that the residents of his street were known as "car line crackers."

They had to accommodate themselves to a vastly changed mode of living. Although my grandmother was able to afford to hire two black women to help her in the kitchen, all of the children were expected to share in the household chores. Daddy was responsible for chopping wood for the stove and for putting the cow out to pasture in one of the neighboring vacant lots. The most comfortable rooms were reserved for paying guests. The children had to wait for their meals until the boarders had been fed; some fifty years later, Daddy vividly recalled a time when he was denied some sliced tomatoes that had been prepared for the boarders.

My grandmother managed for a while to hold on to the property in St. Stephen by selling off small parcels of the land and by borrowing from the bank, but her efforts were futile. The mortgage on the property was ultimately foreclosed on a $1,500 loan for fertilizer. Many years later, Daddy said that the event was so painful to the Rivers family that he determined at the time that he would become a lawyer. When, finally, he did become a lawyer, he attempted—unsuccessfully—to get back some of the St. Stephen property for his mother.

In 1918, my grandmother married Charles Francis Shepard, from Philadelphia, who had been one of the boarders. He had come to North Charleston to help install a dust-collecting system at the asbestos mill. He was drafted into the Army, and after his basic training, before sailing to France, they were married. He was a good deal younger than my grandmother, but their marriage was a long and apparently a happy one. He was a friend to his young stepson and taught Daddy much about the proper use and care of tools, the lessons staying with Daddy throughout his life. Once, when Daddy broke his arm, his stepfather fashioned an ingenious traction device to immobilize his arm as it healed. Grandfather Shepard died in the late 1940s.

"Grandmama Shepard," as I always called her, survived her second husband by many years, living until 1961. I vaguely remember visiting the house on O'Hear Avenue in North Charleston. For just about as long as I can remember, she lived with her daughter Blanche in her house on Sans Souci Street in Charleston, where Aunt Blanche ran Blanche Darby Florist. Daddy and Blanche seemed to have a special kind of relationship and part of it may have stemmed from the fact that he was so appreciative of her taking care of their mother, whom he clearly adored as much as she did him.

Several of Daddy's siblings died quite prematurely when I was a young child. In the summer of 1949, Daddy's eldest sister, Berniece, spent a vacation with her family at Herringstone, the farm Daddy acquired in Virginia in the early 1940s. She enjoyed the farm immensely, as did Daddy, and was driving a tractor when she suffered a fatal heart attack. When she was stricken, Daddy was enroute from California to Charleston to attend his stepfather's funeral services.

A few years later, another sister, Mildred, also died suddenly of a heart attack. She was waiting in line to vote at the time and had just remarked casually to someone about how she intended to vote when she collapsed, dying at the age of 42. Only a few months later, Earle died while Daddy and Mother were in Europe. They were notified of his death at their hotel in Paris.

By a curious twist of fate, my grandmother's family, the McCays, who had been so proud of their property and means, became impoverished over the years. Many relatives turned to my grandmother for assistance and from time to time she managed to find room in her crowded home for them when necessary. Her brother supported himself by selling off tracts of land he had inherited. Pathetically, having lost everything, he took his *first* paying job when he was middle-aged with the Works Progress Administration (WPA) during the Depression, a fact that amazed my father whose upbringing had included a strong work ethic.

Daddy's first job was in 1917 when he was 11 years old. He carried three and a half gallon water buckets for Jamaican laborers who loaded ships at the docks in North Charleston. He always remembered the workers' chant, as he, a skinny boy, struggled with the heavy buckets: "Water, Jack! You oughta be there and half way back!"

It was wartime and the feverish activity at the port terminals must have been exciting for him as the ships were loaded to send soldiers and supplies to Europe. He worked 11 hours a day, six days a week, for 15 cents an hour. His transportation to and from his job was an old box car with makeshift benches.

Varied jobs filled his summers and after-school hours. He delivered newspapers and sometimes worked in a grocery store. Grocery clerks had to be especially versatile then in order to master all of the many chores required in the store's operation. Besides taking orders, assembling and delivering groceries, they had to cut meat, weigh and compute prices without the help of modern scales, stock the shelves, and clean the store after closing hours. An 18 hour workday yielded $2.50.

When time permitted between jobs after school, Daddy would get into some of the organized "sand lot" baseball games held in the neighborhood, undoubtedly one of the few recreations available in the working community of North Charleston at the time. The game opened up a new world for him when he found that he was a pretty good player. He later played in college and, while in law school, played semi-professionally. Ironically, his baseball coach in college was Alfred von Kolnitz, the man who would be his opponent in the Congressional race in 1940.

He never lost his passion for the game. Daddy always enjoyed participating in the annual Congressional Democrat-Republican Baseball Game. A newspaper article in the 1950s once commended Daddy on his batting performance in a Congressional game, but noted that he had failed as an out-fielder to stop a home run hit by Michigan Republican Gerald Ford.

One summer as a teenager, Daddy worked for his neighbor and friend Felix Davis who was the superintendent of the machine shop for GARCO, the asbestos mill. Daddy impressed Mr. Davis a great deal because he would alternate sweeping out the shop every two hours with studying for two hours. My father was one of the few people that he knew in the community who was determined to get an education and succeed beyond the limited opportunities readily available there, a lesson which Mr. Davis emphasized to his own children. They became lifelong friends and Felix Davis was always one of Daddy's greatest champions. He was one of the first to encourage Daddy to enter politics representing North Charleston.

One of Davis' sons was Daddy's namesake and godchild. After my father's death, Mendel Davis succeeded him as First District Congressman. Felix Davis helped campaign and once approached an old friend and told him that his son was running for Congress and asked him to support him. "Well, Felix," the friend replied, "I'll be voting for your son, but you didn't have to tell me that he was running for Congress. I knew the day that you named him Mendel that he'd be running for Congress one of these days."

My grandmother adored my father, "worshipped the dirt under Mendel's feet," according to my Aunt Blanche. She instilled in her young son the necessity of having the essential tools with which to make himself successful in a competitive world. Like her Scottish forebears, she was a stubborn fighter, a quality which my father also possessed.

Daddy came to understand at an early age that hard work would put food on the table, but his mother also emphasized the value of an education and faithful religious practice. For 12 years Daddy was the superintendent for the church Sunday School and served as the Episcopal Diocesan president for the Young People's Service League. Religion was always important to him. With few exceptions, he attended church every Sunday. And, as long as I can remember, he knelt by his bed to say his prayers every evening before retiring.

A student he was not. One of his earliest memories of school was of the two-room school in North Charleston where Sumner Guerry, son of Bishop Guerry, was the teacher. "He read *Little Lord Fauntleroy* to the class, and that started me right off against him," Daddy once said. Mr. Guerry later left his teaching job and joined the Army to go chasing Poncho Villa in Mexico.

As there was no high school in North Charleston, Daddy, in 1920, enrolled in the High School of Charleston, then for boys only. The school, a 45-minute ride by street car from his home, was a foreign land to Daddy. He remembered that some of the tough, older boys sometimes bullied him and, on occasion, even their teachers. Students had to pass every subject in order to be promoted to the next level. It must have been intimidating both socially and academically; Daddy failed algebra and had to repeat the first year.

He did, however, do well in the study of foreign languages, studying French and Spanish, which he enjoyed using throughout his life. Somewhere along the way he acquired some German, as well. And poetry became one of his lifelong interests; he easily memorized long poems and later often dotted his speeches with lines from his favorite poets, especially Robert Burns.

One of his teachers was Hervey Allen, who later became internationally known for his books *Anthony Adverse* and *Israfel, The Life and Times of Edgar Allan Poe*. Charlestonians considered him brilliant, though eccentric. Tall and lanky, he liked to wear cowboy boots and large Western belt buckles. The boys called him Cowboy Allen.

He would, Daddy said, jump up and down on his desk and bellow to the student, "The verb *to be* never takes an object." He would continue to jump. "You think I'm crazy, don't you, boys?"

"Oh, no, sir, Mister Allen," they'd reply.

"Well, just remember, the verb *to be* never takes an object!"

And remember, they did.

Mr. Allen was a founder of the prestigious Poetry Society of South Carolina that was visited by many prominent writers. He and DuBose Heyward, who wrote *Porgy* (whose story became internationally known in the opera *Porgy and Bess*) collaborated on the publication of a book of poetry.

Daddy won his first "political" victory by being elected captain of the volleyball team at the high school. A classmate, Earl Halsall, campaigned for him and lettered elaborate placards saying "Vote for Rivers."

Geometry was one of the requirements for graduation. Unfortunately, Daddy broke his arm during his senior year and, being unable to write the exam, decided to memorize the textbook. His teacher, Fritz Muller, heard his exam and passed him.

He graduated from the High School of Charleston in 1926 at 20 years of age, receiving the only diploma he would ever earn.

Daddy continued to hold various jobs to help support the family, but was determined to carry on with his education and enrolled at the College of Charleston. Hard times might help explain the fact that he did not excel as a student, but he always candidly admitted that, despite his ambition, he was not particularly conscientious at that time. Mr. Edwin DuBose, uncle of DuBose Heyward, was rooming in my grandmother's house during those days and he repeatedly assured her that Daddy would amount to something.

The College of Charleston in 1926 was a small, municipal institution, covering one square block in downtown Charleston. It prided itself on its independence and academic purity in curriculum. Daddy considered his tenure there only as a means to enter law school.

He enjoyed his years at the College, though. Endowed with a natural ability to get along with people, not only one-on-one, but also in large groups, he helped to organize campus activities. He loved to talk and was beginning to grow out of the shyness he had often felt among his peers. Classmates from those years remember him as outgoing and friendly, with a sense of humor and a keen wit. While he still had to work after classes to help the family financially, he was able to find time to socialize and form some strong and lasting friendships...and to play baseball.

By 1929, he had earned enough credits at the College to enter the law school at the University of South Carolina in Columbia. Financially, it was difficult for him, but his family helped him as best they could. Academically, it was particularly frustrating.

"Nobody would have bet a plugged nickel on me then," he said years later. "Even when I knew the assignment, I'd freeze with stage fright. My breath came so short that it was all I could do to say, "Pass me, Professor."

Finally, Dean J. Nelson Frierson called him in for a conference. The dean was kind. "Are any of your people lawyers?" he asked my father.

"No, Sir."

"Well, the faculty doesn't believe that you are cut out to be a lawyer. We don't think that you have the legal aptitude."

"But aren't my written papers good?" my father inquired.

"Yes, they are, but you can't talk or present a case. I'm afraid you'll have to leave the law school. I suggest that you go back to North Charleston and learn a trade. You'll never become a lawyer."

"Well, you'll never be a *real* dean, and I *will* become a lawyer," Daddy *said* he shot back at Dean Frierson.

I think that my father embellished his account of the incident!

He returned to the College of Charleston to take some courses so that he might take the South Carolina Bar examination. It was still permissible to "read" for the Bar exam. (It was not until years later that prospective lawyers had to be graduates of a law school in order to take

15

the exam.)

Daddy achieved more academically that second go-round at the College. His encounter with the dean of the law school had made him ever more determined to pass the Bar exam and to become a lawyer. He was gradually acquiring self-confidence in speaking before crowds. He was active in founding the Bachelor's Club in Charleston and became a campus organizer for the Young Democrats Club.

Sparked by the dynamic personality of Franklin Roosevelt, the politically-charged atmosphere in America in the early 1930s was fertile ground for the organization of political groups. Young Democrats clubs sprang up all over the country, formed with the idealistic goal of active participation in democracy.

Charleston's Young Democrats organization was instigated, in part, through the effort of a College or Charleston professor, José Guillardo, who emphasized to the voters of the future the importance of both national patriotism and states' rights. Daddy, no doubt, was deeply influenced while at the College. The young Democrats on the local level in South Carolina easily merged into the national Young Democrats of America.

Daddy enjoyed participation in political groups. Liking people, his own youthful idealism convinced him that, perhaps through politics, he could develop his abilities and accomplish something. "It was during these years, somewhere along the line, that I definitely made up my mind that I would enter the political field," he recalled many years later.

First, however, he had to become a lawyer, so he diligently read the law books.

One afternoon in the spring of 1932, he was in his mother's back yard chopping wood for the stove when she called to him from the back porch that a letter had just been delivered for him. Recognizing the return address, he quietly opened the envelope with trembling hands. Then he let out a loud, joyful whoop, and hugged his mother. He had passed the Bar exam!

Before too long, he hung out his shingle with Joseph Fromberg on Broad Street in downtown Charleston, where many prestigious law offices were located near the court houses. Many of the well-established lawyers, Daddy quickly realized, had little faith in the young man from, of all places, North Charleston, and would not hire him. He was grateful to Fromberg for allowing him to share the office where he began his practice of law. "Judge" Fromberg, as he liked to be called (having once served as a police recorder or city "judge"), had graduated from the law school at the University of South Carolina in 1910 at the age of 20. A special act of the State Legislature was passed to admit him to the Bar at that young age so that the could practice law.

Almost immediately, Daddy decided to run for political office.

At that time, there were no Representatives from North Charleston in the State House of Representatives. Daddy was encouraged by his friends Felix Davis and Colie Morse to run. Charleston Mayor Burnet Maybank's Democratic party faction controlled politics throughout Charleston County; indeed, it ran things throughout much of the lower part of the state. Daddy paid a visit to the Mayor, seeking his endorsement, but Maybank apparently saw no benefit to his organization in supporting an unknown from North Charleston. He soundly rebuffed him. More determined than ever, Daddy ran as an independent Democrat.

He lost the election.

In 1933, a vacancy occurred in the Charleston County delegation when Representative Ben Scott Whaley resigned to join the Washington staff of U.S. Senator James F. Byrnes. In a special election, Daddy ran and was elected with the campaign slogan "Give the Northern End of the County Representation."

Mayor Maybank's organization did not oppose him when he offered for re-election in 1934. The local Depression economy needed all the federal funding it could acquire. The U.S. Navy Yard was in North Charleston and Daddy was a strong and vocal Roosevelt supporter in those days; perhaps Maybank felt that it was no time to buck one of the incumbents who backed the President.

Daddy received the highest number of votes in the county for the House seats; having led the ticket, he was elected Chairman of the Charleston County delegation.

In Columbia, he served on the Judiciary and Education

Committees, and worked to get an equitable workmen's compensation law on the books. He continued to be extremely active in the Young Democrats, becoming its South Carolina president in 1935, He attended several national conventions, making lasting friendships with Democrats from other parts of the county. One close friend was John Neff of Staunton, Virginia. Mother and Daddy later visited John and Dot Neff on their wedding trip and they would become my Godparents.

The President's son, James Roosevelt, the Young Democrats' national secretary, spoke at the 1935 South Carolina convention in Charleston. Thirty years later when both he and Daddy were serving in the U.S. House of Representatives, he was a neighbor in a residential area in McLean, Virginia.

In 1936, Daddy went for the first time as a delegate to the Democratic National Convention.

There was little doubt, however, that he was setting his sights on South Carolina's First District Congressional seat. It was reported in the Charleston *News and Courier* that he had requested an entry blank from the state Democratic secretary to file for office in 1936.

The incumbent Congressman, Thomas McMillan, had served since 1926. It was apparently no secret, though, that McMillan had somewhat lost touch with his constituency. Daddy and Judge Fromberg met with McMillan and discussed the upcoming election. Daddy must have appeared to be at least a potential threat to McMillan, who was not ready to give up his seat in Congress; shortly after the meeting, both Fromberg and Daddy were offered positions in the U.S. Department of Justice, jobs which McMillan used his influence to help procure.

My father realized that experience in Washington would be invaluable to his future in national politics, especially if McMillan looked upon him as a possible successor. He was also realistic: the Justice Department job meant a steady income of around $3200 a year, unlike the precarious and competitive practice of law in Charleston and the minuscule salary of a state legislator. He accepted the assignment with enthusiasm.

Daddy moved to Washington late in 1936 and worked in several Divisions of the Justice Department, including Anti-Trust, Criminal and Bond & Spirits. After about two years, he was asked to undertake some specific projects which required a great deal of travelling in many states in the South.

For much of the time he worked with Jackson B. Love, then an investigator with the Department. Their job, within the Taxes and Penalties Division, was to attempt to collect unpaid criminal fines and forfeited criminal bail bonds that were carried on the books of the various U.S. District Clerks' offices. It was a new activity for the Justice Department and Daddy and Mr. Love dealt not only with law enforcement officers but often with the convicted felon or the bail bond debtor.

"Times were pretty hard in those days and money was really scarce," Mr. Love told me. "Mendel had some authority affecting individual human lives in collecting money but he never forgot to be human and understanding and kind. He told me once that a person must be firm and do a duty but one should never forget that a person can only give what they have to give. He told me one day, after a hot session with a couple of debtors, 'in the end you are only you.' I vividly remember these statements, even after the passing of half a century."

He even recalled a toast which Daddy gave in 1938 (at Jack and Polly Love's engagement dinner) that he felt indicated some of the philosophy towards life that Mendel Rivers held: "We come into this world all naked and bare. We go thru this world beset with care. We go out of this world to only God knows where. If you were a thoroughbred here, you will be a thoroughbred there."

"We were single, unmarried young men. While working in New Orleans, we shared a bedroom in a private home and especially enjoyed the good food of the city and seldom objected to 'wetting our whistle' once in a while. However, I repeat money was scarce and in that era 'money' was not freely spent...It should be remembered that the minimum wage invoked under President Roosevelt was a whopper of 25 cents per hour and *that* was money in those days."

CHAPTER 2

In the summer of 1930, Margaret Middleton went to Hendersonville, North Carolina, to visit her friend Jane Register. This part of North Carolina has long been a popular vacation area for Charlestonians seeking an escape from the humid Lowcountry summers. One afternoon she and Jane drove over to Kanuga, the nearby Episcopal Church retreat, to see friends from Charleston who were staying there.

Daddy was attending a conference of the Young People's Service League being held at Kanuga.

"The only person I remember talking to that afternoon was Mendel Rivers. I was greatly impressed by the tall, soft-spoken stranger, and by his prestige among the other campers...he had just been elected the Best Boy Camper," Mother recalled. Later, Daddy often wondered how in the world he could have been elected the best *boy* camper when he was 24 years old and a student in law school.

A year later Mother was a freshman at the College of Charleston where she again met Mendel Rivers: "I recall seeing him often at the 'Cistern,' a favorite gathering place for students between classes. He had friendly greetings for all, though he seemed to me to be a quiet, serious type."

They had one date that year, which, to Mother's recollection, was not a great success. They rode around the Boulevard facing the harbor and through Hampton Park in his coupé, and he held her hand, but the conversation lagged for the most part. They went to a "drive-in" restaurant across the Ashley River for a "Dope and a Bozo," popular slang of the day for Coca-Cola and a snack.

From the beginning, he always called her Marguerite, rather than Margaret. Mother said that she never really knew why. And he never called her "Marwee," the nickname her family and childhood friends used.

In 1938 while working for the Justice Department in the Southern states, Daddy was able to spend more time in Charleston. In the spring of that year he and Mother met again at a tea dance at the Country Club.

Mother remembered: "In the several years since I had last seen him, he seemed to have gained enormous charm, self-confidence and sophistication. I was pleased that, within days, he began calling me for dates."

At the time, she was working at the Charleston *Evening Post* as the Assistant Society Editor, a position she had held for over a year. Prior to that she had taught school in rural Sumter County, about a hundred miles from Charleston. Her teaching salary had been $75 per month, for nine months of the school year, but, in those Depression days, she had been thankful to have it and be able to afford the $1 per day for room and board.

When she returned to Charleston, she again lived with her parents at 24 New Street where she, the eldest child, had grown up with her brother Charlie and sister Dorothy. My grandfather, Charles Middleton, was a cotton exporter, a business that he and his brothers Abbott and Gus had operated with their father for many years. The Middleton and Company wharf on the Cooper River was one of the largest and most active in the South during its lifetime. Two other Middleton brothers, Tom and Willoughby, left Charleston to study law and both eventually settled in the New York area.

My grandparents' home always delighted me. It is a big house built in the 1870s by "a notorious Scalawag," I was told, even before I was able to understand the disreputable implication. My grandparents' bedroom was what had been designed as a ballroom by the infamous first owner. In the late 1940s, the house was converted into apartments by my grandparents who occupied the spacious one on the first floor. For many years, Dick Reeves, whose gift as a raconteur of stories in the Lowcountry black patois, Gullah, lived in the upstairs apartment. It was a special treat to be allowed to go upstairs and visit him. He helped to popularize and preserve this unique heritage and entertained people all over the country with his tales—even in the White House.

In 1930, Mother's beloved grandfather, known affectionately as "Fanfan," came to live in his eldest son's home at 24 New Street. He had found the other children's homes not suitable. Mother learned long after the fact that he was horrified that his granddaughter had accepted a paying job after finishing college. To his mind, a lady should live with her parents and be supported by them until she married and was then to be taken care of by her husband. Fanfan died in 1939 at the age of 80 soon after the birth of my sister, his first great grandchild.

Mother said that she never felt particularly prosperous growing up. The cotton market went up and down constantly and, she says, "the Middleton men spent lavishly when times were good but frequently there was no money when the bills came due. We were never impoverished, but never rich, either." The mistress of the household, my grandmother, welcomed the universal poverty of the Depression with the remark: "Well, thank goodness, things are getting back to normal!"

Grandmother Middleton liked Daddy from the very beginning when he first appeared at her door in his baseball uniform. "He was embarrassed, but she was very much impressed," Mother remembered. "She *always* adored Mendel and could find little fault with him."

His courtship of Mother was whirlwind. And it was also somewhat unorthodox. Once he arrived bearing a bushel of corn, and another time, with a German Shepherd puppy.

One day, he casually tossed a carton of cigarettes into Mother's lap after picking her up from work.

"Oh, Mendel," she exclaimed, "you are a darling! How thoughtful of you!" She was impressed by his generosity since she could only afford one pack at a time on her salary of $17 a week.

"Glad you like them," he replied. "Now, I hope you'll quit smoking."

Daddy experimented with smoking but grew to dislike it intensely. My sister remembers, as a small child, seeing him put out a cigarette and announce that he would never smoke another one. He never did. And he barely tolerated smoking by others in later years.

Mother quit smoking after they had been married about 15 years; mainly, she said, because Daddy made life utterly miserable for her when she smoked. Even if she had aired out the house hours before his arrival home, he'd storm in saying, "Who's been smoking those dirty, nasty, filthy, stinking cigarettes?"

He once telephoned a friend who had sent him a handsome ashtray and said: "It's right here on my office desk and I thank you for sending me such a fine ashtray for this room. It looks perfect here. Of course," he added, "I never smoke myself. I can't stand the damned things. But if any fool wants to kill himself here in this office, I'll see that he does it First Class."

Daddy and Mother frequently dined at Henry's, a popular restaurant in the Market area of Charleston. They also enjoyed sailing with friends in the harbor and spending afternoons on the beach on Sullivan's Island, where many families including my grandparents, had summer homes. My grandmother was told by a friend that she had seen Margaret and Mendel waiting in line to pay the 25-cents toll to cross the Cooper River Bridge, adding, "I knew they were in love. They were smiling at each other, and how else could people be smiling so happily when they have to pay a toll?"

One afternoon, Daddy and Mother drove out to Folly Beach to visit his mother who was vacationing there with his sister Blanche. He suggested taking his mother for a drive. As they got into the car, he abruptly announced: "Muth, Marguerite and I are going to get married!" Mother recalls that she was horrified at the way he surprised his mother with such important and personal news, "but without hesitation, Mrs. Shepard reached over and touched my hand and said, 'Oh, that's wonderful!' I will always remember how gracious she was. I was very lucky...I never had a cross word with my mother-in-law."

The engagement was announced on June 28, 1938.

Daddy spent most of that summer travelling. The Justice

23

Department job kept him on the road, but he was also campaigning enthusiastically for Congressman McMillan who had suffered a heart attack. Mother said that it wa a wonderful and exciting summer planning her wedding. They wrote each other long and loving letters when out of town and spent every possible hour together then he was in town.

Several times during that summer Mother accompanied Daddy on his trips around the First Congressional District. On one occasion they travelled to Hampton County to attend a political rally where he spoke on behalf of McMillan in the small community of Grays. After stopping in the town of Hampton to have supper with Mr. and Mrs. Eugene Peeples, they followed their host's car down a dirt road for some 15 miles, swallowing mouthfuls of dust most of the way. The small school house in Grays was jam-packed with a sleepy, perspiring audience. Children were squirming in the audience and in cars parked outside.

Daddy wanted to catch McMillan's opponent, Russell McGowan, off guard. For what seemed an eternity, Mother and Daddy waited outside while McGowan spoke. Finally, Mr. Peeples got up and announced that Mendel Rivers had come all the way from Charleston to speak for Congressman McMillan.

Mother was impressed by her fiancé that evening. "During the speech, Mendel and McGowan had a heated exchange and I was certain that a fight was imminent. I felt that if such a thing had happened, that I surely would have rushed to Mendel's physical defense. But I learned a lot about politics that evening. Following the talk, McGowan came up to Mendel and me and was most cordial; he and Mendel even had a drink together, as though nothing had happened. It was as though they had been putting on an act.

"At the time, of course, I had no idea that Mendel would be campaigning for himself within two years. In retrospect, I was amazingly naive. It wasn't difficult to see how much Mendel enjoyed the atmosphere of politics and campaigning, and that he was very good at it. He instinctively knew how to get along with people, and could be agreeable and charming even with his opponents."

Mother has admitted that she should have known what she was getting into.

My parents were married on September 1, 1938. When they turned from the altar to walk down the aisle of St. Michael's Episcopal Church, she looked up at him adoringly but he was not gazing at his new bride.

"Recognizing guests in the crowded pews," Mother remembered, "he smiled and greeted them cordially as we progressed to the rear of the church. In the vestibule, he spoke to late arrivals and introduced me as 'Mrs. Rivers.' Even after seating me in the waiting limousine, Mendel continued to shake hands with well-wishers."

Even at his own wedding, Daddy was in his element. Mother had married a consummate politician.

After the wedding reception, held in my grandparents' home, the couple left in Daddy's Chrysler and drove across the Cooper River Bridge, paying the 25-cents toll. The first piece of legislation that Daddy had written several years before as a member of the S.C. Legislature was one to eliminate the toll, but the bill had not passed.

Before they had gone far, they stopped to visit Congressman Tom McMillan, who was recuperating from the heart attack he had suffered, at his home on Sullivan's Island.

They headed for Myrtle Beach, intending to stay at the elegant Ocean Forest Hotel, then the only first class hotel there. When they drove up to the entrance, after dark, they were astonished to find the place in total darkness.

"Maybe the power is out," Daddy suggested.

Almost immediately a man with a flashlight appeared by their car. "What's the matter?" Daddy demanded. "We want to stay here for the night."

"Sorry, Mister," the watchman replied, "this place closed down yesterday...end of the season."

Mother said that Daddy, angry with himself, muttered some profanity and wearily turned his car around to search for less imposing accommodations.

They spent a fortnight on their wedding trip in North Carolina, Virginia and Washington.

Daddy's work with the Department of Justice continued to require a great deal of travelling. His first assignment after his marriage was in

Macon, Georgia.

Mother was impressed: "I knew Mendel was important. His business card revealed that he was 'Special Assistant to the Attorney General of the United States.' I was sure that the Attorney General had searched diligently to find such an accomplished lawyer to work for him."

En route to Macon, they were appalled by the bad roads and extreme poverty that they encountered in Georgia. Conditions seemed worse than in South Carolina which was distressed and shabby enough itself in those Depression days. The highways were full of potholes and in many place along the way farmers tried to hail them down to sell large bags of pecans or other products for a dollar.

They stayed in a hotel in Macon until they could find more reasonably priced quarters. The hotel "was terribly expensive at $4 a day," Mother wrote to her parents. "We tramped through town yesterday. There were plenty of tourist homes and boarding houses, but they were pathetic relics of decayed splendor, all kept by shabby women and were furnished atrociously, with linoleum rugs, hopeless wallpaper and hideous furniture. We got so desperate that we went to the only wealthy-looking one on one street. Mendel asked if there was a room to rent. The haughty maid replied disdainfully, 'Only rich aristocratic people live here!' as she quickly closed the door...We found the place we're in now that way, however. There is only an old lady and she is very good to us. The room is five dollars a week, and we have a private bath...Please send me my bath towels as these are pretty thin...

"Macon is pleasant. Everyone is friendly and hospitable to us. At church today, several people introduced themselves, and one lady even offered to take us home in her car. How chilly St. Michael's must seem to visitors..."

After several months in Macon, Daddy was assigned to Atlanta, and my parents sublet an apartment with the first kitchen in which to prepare their own meals since they had married. Mother admitted that much of the cooking actually fell to Daddy who was accomplished in that field, having been a bachelor for a long time. Mother had grown up in a household where the mistress of the house went into the kitchen only to instruct the cook. I am sure that my grandmother thought that her daughter would have many servants after she married. Mother said that at the time of her marriage she knew how to make lemon meringue pie and oyster stew.

She read cookbooks diligently and one day she searched in vain for instructions. Finally, in frustration, she called Daddy at his office and asked: "Mendel, how do you bake a potato? Should the oven be hot or cold when you start?"

"My God, Marguerite!" he exclaimed. "Just *cook* the damned potato."

After many other short term assignments in Georgia and Tennessee, they moved to Washington in June of 1939. In less than ten months of marriage, they had lived in 39 different places.

By that time, Mother was six months pregnant. In those days, a lady, quite literally, was not supposed to appear in public once her pregnancy became evident. The subject was never even discussed in mixed company. She remembered feeling particularly enormous when a tactless acquaintance insisted that twins must be imminent. "I felt especially tremendous one warm afternoon," Mother recalled, "when Mendel and I went to the Department of Justice building to watch a welcoming parade on Pennsylvania Avenue for the King and Queen of England. As we crowded into one of the window areas, I knew that the other attorneys and their wives wished I were elsewhere. The 'Imminent Arrival' and I took up a great amount of the coveted space...all for a fleeting glimpse of the royal couple." (Many years later Daddy and I met the former Queen whom he had seen from a distance in 1939. In the summer of 1970, the Queen Mother hosted a garden party in London, as part of activities commemorating the 300th anniversary of the settling of Charles Towne.)

Mother said that when they were back in Washington at that time that she made a belated discovery: *all* the attorneys in the Department of Justice were "Special Assistants to the Attorney General of the United States." Daddy confessed to her that the title had once misled him, too.

Because Daddy's work required that he be available to travel, their stay in Washington was much too unsettled, so they decided that Mother should return to Charleston and stay with her parents until the baby arrived—a decision with which her two obstetricians agreed. Daddy wined and dined her for a week at some of Washington's best restaurants before her departure. It was a sad parting when Daddy put her on the train at Union Station. She wept copiously when he was out of sight. It was her 26th birthday.

Mother settled in with her family and made clothes for the baby as the steamy weeks of a Charleston summer dragged on. Daddy finally joined her late in August. On the night of September 1, 1939, Daddy awakened her excitedly as he listened to a radio news broadcast.

"Listen to this, Marguerite. History is being made. Hitler has entered Poland." It was their first anniversary.

Three weeks later their first child, my sister Margaret, called Peggy, arrived.

Less than a week later Daddy casually dropped the bombshell!

Paying his customary daily visit to Mother in the hospital, he abruptly announced:

"Marguerite, Tom McMillan died today."

"Oh, that's too bad." Mother responded.

"I'm going to run for Congress," he added.

"Oh, Mendel," she protested, "you're not really going to do *that*, are you?"

"I surely am, just as soon as Mrs. McMillan has finished serving out his unexpired term."

Mother's pleas were to no avail. At the time, she could not believe that Daddy would undertake such a risky and ambitious project. She felt overwhelmed, but he couldn't be dissuaded.

And, even though she had been scheduled to leave the hospital the next day, she broke out into a rash (caused, she was firmly convinced, by his announcement) and she and my sister remained in the hospital for several more days.

He clung to his desire to run for Congress and realized early on that he would be coming up against a powerful Democratic political establishment. Alfred "Fritz" von Kolnitz, who was in the insurance business in Charleston, reportedly was going to run for the office and had the backing of Charleston's mayor, Henry W. Lockwood (nicknamed

"Tunker") and South Carolina's Governor, Burnet Maybank, the former mayor of Charleston. Maybank and Lockwood had been political allies for a number of years, and, not unlike many places in the country, held the reins controlling most political activity in lower South Carolina.

Daddy was often assigned to jobs closer to home during that fall and early winter. For many weeks he worked in South Carolina.

From Columbia, Daddy wrote to Mother: "There were people from all over the District at the football game yesterday, and I really got in some politicking. Fritz von Kolnitz had Tom McMillan worried. He'll cause me worry in the end, too. I saw him sitting in Maybank's box at the game."

CHAPTER 3

Charleston, South Carolina, in 1940, was a relatively quiet Southern city. One of the few great American cities before the Civil War, she clung ferociously to her pride, aristocratic heritage and traditions, in large part, because she had lost everything else by 1865. The grand and elegant eighteenth and nineteenth century homes fronting the harbor and lining the streets belied the conditions that existed. In parts of the city there was no money to even pave the streets. Like everyone else in the Depression-plagued country, she was poor, but in the South that meant just a little bit poorer.

Railroad freight rates which were undeniably discriminatory had been imposed on the Southern states following the Civil War and had caused a lingering economic malady. The ups and downs of the waning cotton industry could not be counted upon to provide any prospects of future wealth. Goods being shipped through the once-prosperous port were down to a trickle. And after the Crash of 1929, the Northern capital dried up that was necessary to things like the state's truck farming industry and the beginnings of a tourist trade.

In the early years of the Depression, the city government's money had disappeared when the People's National Bank failed. Along with many other places in the country, Charleston was forced to resort to paying its municipal workers with script.

But there was nothing impoverished about the political machine running the city. Throughout the century, Charleston had had especially powerful mayors who were able to wield great influence over the city's affairs, sometimes for the betterment of the city but always for the betterment of their own and their friends' political futures. It was said that, in statewide elections, Charleston's votes were reported last so that the vote counters could turn in what was needed to win the election.

Mayor Burnett Rhett Maybank capitalized on this tradition. Descended from some of Charleston's earliest settlers, he was a member of Charleston's social elite. He was also a political master. He was able to bring the city out of its financial depths within just two years by cutting budgets and salaries and by other creative means. Charleston, unlike the Bible Belt upstate, had long had an "understanding" with liquor dealers and with the madams running the brothels. Maybank was also able to take advantage of his friendship with then Junior Senator James F. Byrnes, who was instrumental in obtaining federal funding for some of Maybank's favorite projects.

Maybank used his skilled and excellent powers of persuasion to get the state legislature to enact a law which allowed the mayor to appoint the city's police commissioner. Equally important, he also began the policy of annual appointments of city employees.

When Maybank was elected South Carolina's Governor in 1938, his well-entrenched political machine remained intact in Charleston. Alderman (Councilman) Henry W. Lockwood was elected by the city's council to serve out Maybank's term and he subsequently was elected in 1939 to a full four-year term as Mayor. A former tugboat captain, "Tunker" Lockwood had thoroughly learned from Maybank how the game was played.

Mendel Rivers was not a member of this political club. He was, among other things, an outsider, from, of all places, *North* Charleston. There still exists a certain great divide, whether real or imagined, between downtown, old Charleston and the areas to the north of it— socially, culturally and politically. And in 1940, it was more real than imagined.

When my father, after passing the bar exam, had knocked on the doors of many Broad Street lawyers looking for a job, he had been soundly rebuffed. His mother, who was distantly related to many of the

31

prominent members of the legal profession, had accompanied him, hoping to help him get a foot in the door. It made no difference.

When he had gone to then Mayor Maybank in 1932 to ask for his support in a race for the state legislature, Maybank had turned him down, seeing no reason at all to offer him support. My father had run against the machine as an independent then, but lost the race. A year later he ran again when a vacancy occurred and won, but still without Maybank's endorsement.

My father announced his candidacy for Congressman in February of 1940.

There was no doubt in anyone's mind who was slated to win the election—and it was not Mendel Rivers.

Alfred "Fritz" von Kolnitz was the candidate of choice of both Mayor Lockwood and Governor Maybank. He had a lot of power behind him. Some considered him a weakling and a pawn in the political machine's hands, but few considered anything but total victory for him.

Perhaps the most incredible aspect of von Kolnitz' candidacy was his name. That someone with such a German-sounding name would be put forth for public office just as Hitler was on a rampage in Europe seems, in retrospect, to have been unbelievably short-sighted.

Just before his announcement to run, Daddy told my mother:

"I honestly believe that I can beat von Kolnitz. The mere fact that the *Great* Lockwood and the *Grand* Maybank are jointly supporting him does not scare me in the slightest."

It scared my mother a great deal. It was not a prospect that she looked forward to as a relatively new wife and mother of a four-month old. For one thing, Daddy was forced to resign from his job with the U.S. Justice Department in order to run for Congress. The newly-enacted Hatch Act prohibited Federal employees from campaigning for offices in the Federal government.

Mother was not a complete stranger to politics although it was never her natural inclination. Her father, Charles Middleton, had served as a city alderman under Maybank and had been appointed the police commissioner by Lockwood. Socially and politically in the same camp with Maybank, my grandfather was civic-minded and enjoyed any services he could render to the city. His position as police commissioner was, of course, voluntary and he proudly considered himself to be totally non-partisan.

If my father had anticipated any assistance from Tom McMillan's widow, Clara, because of his association with her husband, he was sadly mistaken.

Von Kolnitz was closely allied with the McMillans. It was even rumored that he had had an affair with a sister-in-law of McMillan.

In a letter dated August 16, 1940, Mrs. McMillan wrote to my father's opponent:

"Dear Alfred:

In reference to your telephone call today, I have obtained information from the Justice Department covering the points you listed:

1. Nature of employment—appointed Associate Attorney ($3200), Taxes and Penalties Unit, Justice, October, 1936; transferred...

2. Whether of not he was Assistant to the Attorney General—No. He was never at any time connected with the office of the Attorney General.

3. How many men employed in a similar capacity at that time—about a thousand.

In regard to Mendel's appeal to the Executive Committee, I feel very strongly that he should be permitted to have watchers at all the polls in order to forestall any charges of corruption, which charges he has declared he will press if he is not elected. While I do not want you to think I am trying to dictate to the Committee or even advise them and while I am not thoroughly familiar with the rules governing watchers, I am trying to look at the matter from the point of view of the average voter. If he is refused watchers, naturally, the impression will be that the polls are machine-handled. Publicity of this nature would of course give Charleston another blackeye and,

I am afraid, might possibly reflect on your popularity
among your supporters...
I have received several more very favorable replies to the letter I
have written about you..."

My father, when he went to Washington after the election, was
assigned the same office that Mrs. McMillan had used and, for a while,
he employed the same secretary. This letter was apparently discovered
in the files left behind by Mrs. McMillan.

Not long after Daddy's election, he assisted Mrs. McMillan in
unravelling the red tape involved in getting the Federal pension to
which she was entitled, and interceded on her behalf in securing a position with a Federal agency.

Most of the established politicians opposed him. He was 34 years
old and, although he had served in the State Legislature, he was considered, among other things, to be too young to be the Congressman. He
memorized several passages by and about famous young Americans so
that he could fire back at opponents who regarded him as a boyish contender. In many speeches, he would remind his listeners: "Jefferson,
incidentally, wrote the Declaration of Independence at the age of 33..."

The odds were impressive. Everyone, including Daddy, knew that
he had only an outside chance of winning that election. However, as was
his nature, he was unremittingly optimistic. And, many people were
becoming discontented with the existing political establishment.

Daddy was fortunate in having many loyal friends, and he sought
the support of everyone he knew and found it sometimes in unexpected
quarters.

Jack Maybank, a brother of the Governor, was a particularly special
friend of Daddy's and gave him much encouragement by making the
first financial contribution to the campaign. In addition, my grandfather
Middleton was Godfather to one of Jack Maybank's triplet sons.

Even some of the Mayor's longtime supporters decided to go with
Daddy. Early in the campaign he visited Mitch Robinson, a businessman
prominent in the Jewish community and in local politics, to ask for his
help. Robinson's son, Irving, remembered Daddy's visit to the Robinson
bicycle store on upper King Street.

"Mendel came in and they talked for a while and then my father got on the phone and called Lockwood and asked him to support Mendel Rivers. When the Mayor said emphatically that he would not, my father hung up the phone and promptly called all of his Jewish friends to back Mendel."

One of his most enthusiastic Jewish supporters over the years was Moses Prystowsky, the owner of a men's clothing store. The friendship extended beyond the political and over a couple of generations: unable to decorate a Christmas tree at home, Mr. Prystowsky's grandson visited the Rivers household for several years to help with the tree trimming.

Denied any help from the establishment, Daddy ran as an independent Democrat against the Charleston-based machine. But he knew how to turn a disadvantage into an advantage. He worked to become a strong candidate in the other eight counties of the district. He constantly urged the voters to exert their own independence by voting against his opponent, who had been selected by the big city bosses of the Charleston regime. Having lived in the country and in a small working man's village, he easily identified himself with people in rural and less sophisticated circumstances, an identity he never lost.

Early in the campaign, Daddy spoke at a rally in Walterboro, a small town some fifty miles from Charleston in the southern part of the district. Joe Riley, Sr., Daddy's long-time friend, supporter and campaign treasurer for many years, told me that from the very start Daddy knew how to gain the upper hand. When Daddy got up to speak, he looked around the crowd and calmly said to the people assembled: "I see that the Mayor of Charleston, along with the Charleston Chief of Police, have come down here to this meeting. Now, I ask you, who do you want as your Congressman in Washington, someone who speaks for you or someone who answers to the Mayor of Charleston?"

The effect was not lost on the voters.

Von Kolnitz was a mild and apparently unimaginative contender who could not ad lib and speak extemporaneously as Daddy could. Mother recalled that it seemed that von Kolnitz had only one speech, albeit memorized, which always deplored the war in Europe. He would cite the tragedy he had recently witnessed in England where small children had been outfitted with gas masks, but the words came out sounding like "goss mosks." He had a formal and stylized manner of speaking, coupled with something of a Boston accent, acquired when he had studied at Harvard.

He alarmed many of the people at campaign meetings. A man in a small town once told Mother: "That von Collins fellow has his nerve; he still speaks with a German accent."

Von Kolnitz was driven to the political "stump" meetings accompanied by the police band of Charleston, which played rousing, patriotic tunes that were designed to appeal to the emotions of the listeners. Mother was told that other policemen were sent to various counties armed with liquor and money to drum up votes.

Daddy appealed to the voter's sense of fair play: "I do not believe that it is left to the discretion of the Honorable Henry W. Lockwood, mayor of Charleston, to decide whether or not I am qualified for the position of your Congressman...I feel that Mr. Lockwood is unwise, as well as unfair, in participating so actively in this campaign for Congress...We have good reasons to suspect that intimidation, through the police and detective departments, is one of the weapons being used against me, and if this method is carried to its logical conclusion, every office in this country will have to pass the censorship of our honorable mayor, and receive his blessing before such an office could be filled. Therefore, for Mr. Lockwood or anyone else to try to assume dictatorial powers will lead to anarchy and totalitarianism."

Von Kolnitz defended himself as the Mayor's choice by publicly asking: "...What degree of cooperation will the citizens of Charleston get from a man who condemns their mayor, their city council...and through inference, the entire citizenship of Charleston. If I go to Washington I intend to retain their friendship and work for the betterment of all...[And he added that] the mayor is my friend. We grew up together.

"I know Charleston. I know Charleston's problems," von Kolnitz told the voters. "I know Charleston and I know the problems of the First congressional district. I tell you, I should go to Washington because I know Charleston."

Daddy campaigned in a new red Chrysler, a novel color for automobiles at that time. When the muffler developed a hole, his sister Blanche begged him not to drive the car, convinced he was courting danger by driving such a conspicuous car throughout the counties. Daddy laughed and replied, "No, I want to be heard. I want all the district to say 'Here comes Rivers in his *Blitzkrieg*.'"

He sped along into the campaign. But things were getting rough.

One evening the Chief of Police called Daddy at home and told him: "Get out of this race or we'll get you out." Mother stood by, aghast at Daddy's response: "Mendel shouted threatening and insulting words, mostly about the chief's lineage, and ended with 'YOU COME NEAR ME AND I'LL KILL YOU.'"

Not long before that, the newspaper had described in horrifying detail the account of four criminals who had stretched a chain across a country road and had brutally attacked the occupants of the first car that they stopped. Mother said that she had horrid visions of the fate that awaited Daddy the next time he sallied forth in his bright new red Chrysler.

Amazingly, they heard no more from the Chief of Police.

One afternoon, however, Mother was driving her father's office car around the Boulevard when a policeman drove up beside her and told her to pull over.

"What's the matter, Officer?" she asked.

"Get that Rivers sticker off your car," he said gruffly.

"Why should I?" she asked.

"'Cause it's the wrong sign, see?"

She mustered up her courage and replied firmly, "Well, *I* think it's the right sign."

"O.K., lady, I'll let you off this time, but don't use it no more, see?"

The policeman had no idea that her husband was the candidate nor that she was the daughter of the Police Commissioner.

My grandfather enjoyed being the Police Commissioner. He had initiated several worthwhile programs for the policemen in target practice, uniform regulations and sick leave compensation. The police had taken him on specially-arranged tours where even the roughest parts of town had been made safe and tidy for his inspection. He could not believe Daddy's assertions that his friends on the police force were working against his son-in-law. But Mother's experiences and other reports finally convinced him that his instructions for neutrality in the election had been ignored. Worse, he realized that he had been used only as a figurehead.

A month before the election, Grandfather protested to the Mayor in person and in an exchange of letters, voiced his complaints:"...When I accepted, I had no idea that you would consider that one of the duties of the police department would be to bend every effort, and a very large part of their energies, in political work. My understanding is that the idea of creating a Commission to handle the affairs of the police department was to remove all activities of the police, as far as possible, from politics.

"I called on you...to make a protest...but you told me that while you were sympathetic regarding my position, you could do nothing about it and that was the proper way to run politics—that when you endorsed a candidate you never did it halfway.

"...I am of the unalterable opinion that the department is the property of the taxpayers of the city of Charleston, and that its purpose is to protect the life, rights and property of the people of our community, and should not be exploited in the interest of partisan politics."

Grandfather's position was made clear for all the voters to see when the exchange of letters between him and Mayor Lockwood was released to and published by Charleston's newspaper, the *News and Courier*. The Mayor defended himself by blaming Daddy for making "thoughtless" accusations throughout the district: "...In all fairness to myself I must point out that the issue has been raised solely by your son-in-law...

"Now, Charlie, you know that the boys in the Charleston Police Department have always been active, individually, in politics. Not while they were on duty but in their off hours, and I think this condition will always be the same...After receiving your letter I telephoned the Police Department and ordered all stickers taken down in headquarters or from city-owned cars, if there are any such stickers on city-owned cars as you seem to think.

"...In your letter you say that the police ought to see that it is a fair election. The Police Department has nothing to do with the running of an election. Police, as you should know, are not allowed within 100 feet of the polls except when called by managers. This, I can assure you, will be the condition at the coming election."

My grandfather resigned his position as Police Commissioner. Mother said that she, wrapped up in the campaign, did not appreciate her father's personal sacrifice at the time.

Thereafter, the Charleston police force contented itself with pulling down Rivers placards from the trees and telephone poles throughout the nine counties.

Palmer Gaillard, who would later serve as Charleston's mayor for 16 years, said that he got an early taste of politics when he was asked by Mother's cousin, Sammy Hasell, to help out in the campaign. The two young men drove around in Palmer's Model-T Ford putting up Rivers posters in the Charleston area. They quickly learned that about as fast as they could put them up, the opposition forces would tear them down. Ever more determined, they began to "replace" von Kolnitz signs when they found that their efforts on behalf of Daddy had been tampered with. "We were once caught in the act of pulling down a von Kolnitz sign," said Palmer, "and were threatened with arrest. Nothing came of it; so we continued the practice."

Daddy even later confessed that he and a stalwart friend, Leo Simonin, carried rakes in their car as they travelled around the district and they, too, tore down the von Kolnitz posters they encountered.

Since he could not afford a secretary at the going rate of $7 per week, Daddy asked Mother to work in the little office that he had rented on Broad Street. A friend, Jimmy Lamb, frequently gave invaluable help by working with Mother to compose speeches, based on outlines suggested by Daddy. While Daddy preferred making unrehearsed speeches, a local law required that a written one be submitted ahead of time.

On one occasion, when Jimmy was not available, Mother and my grandmother Middleton toiled together to produce a speech for a radio address. They thought it was remarkably forceful—and it was. Fortunately, however, Daddy's friend, Leon Patat, came over to read the finished product. He read it through, then commented: "This is a fine and accurate speech, but it would be political suicide. You just cannot say 'Our Mayor is a liar and a cheat.'" He helped to revise their efforts.

Mother's sister Dorothy recorded in her diary that "Marwee and Mendel are both nearly dead with this campaign. They have such terrible odds to fight...[They] haven't got any money to speak of, and very few people to really work for them. I went down to the office yesterday to help out. It's a mad rush. Don't see how Marwee stands it. She's lost a lot of weight and can't sleep...It tears my heart out to see Marwee, Mother and Mendel working so terrifically at this campaign...Marwee looks like a wreck. She works hard all day...Mendel does twice as much as she does...They seem quite hopeful, though."

By now a master in public speaking, Daddy could employ sarcasm in a speech with the timing and sting of a professional entertainer. Since von Kolnitz had served as the City's Playground Commissioner, Daddy frequently derided his opponent's qualifications:

"I believe that the people of this First Congressional District already know that he has not had one day of legislative experience, and that his public service has principally been confined to the perfunctory pastime of maintaining the upkeep of the playgrounds of the city, and overseeing the general welfare of the monkeys and other curiosities confined in the cages at Hampton Park Zoo."

But it was not, of course, the qualifications and experience of Fritz von Kolnitz that Daddy was up against. He knew it, as did everyone else. It has been my impression that he personally liked von Kolnitz. Daddy's speeches reiterated his pleas that the voters support him and break the Charleston regime. One time, he reminded the voters of just how confident the Mayor of Charleston was about the outcome of elections. "Does my opponent consider it dignified...when the mayor of Charleston stated in the early spring at the 25th wedding anniversary of the Honorable Bert Rogers, clerk of court of Beaufort, in the presence of the mayor of Beaufort and other prominent persons, and in *my* presence, that in Charleston a magic wand can be waved over the ballot boxes, so that the votes could come out as desired?

"I leave these questions for your consideration. I know he will not answer them."

Patronage in city jobs was one major key to much of the power that local ward and precinct bosses possessed. Loyalty to the regime meant life-saving jobs for a large segment of the population. Daddy likened the Charleston power bosses to Hitler's gestapo, saying that if "city employees didn't stay in line on election day, they'd soon have to be standing in a bread line."

Local ward bosses could effectively control the vote also through denying a "minority" candidate poll watchers on election day to protect his interests. A few days before the election, at a campaign meeting at Johnson Hagood Stadium, Daddy advised the crowd of several hundreds: "Vote early and avoid the rush. If you vote after 4 [p.m.], you won't vote in some places...This is a federal election. When the stealing begins, they'd better watch out...All we want is a square election. A square election, and I am your congressman...You know that I am qualified, regardless of what the mayor thinks...I'll be most happy to debate the mayor on any stump in the United States on my qualifications—and his."

Election Day arrived, August 27.

Daddy left early in the day to vote and to make rounds at all of the polling places. Mother remained at home until a frightened volunteer, a young man in Daddy's office, telephoned her. A strange, belligerent man had come into the office, he said. In addition, he had seen the Governor across the street from the office, accompanied by a bodyguard with a pistol prominently displayed. Should he close the office, he asked her.

"I immediately departed for Mendel's office with our German Shepherd, a pistol, a bottle of bourbon and a Bible—so that I'd be prepared for any emergency," she recalled. "Luckily, none was needed."

Later in the afternoon, Mother's sister Dorothy called to ask her to ride with her to take a voter to Burke High School, the Ward 12 voting place.

As they were about to leave the school, Mother saw one of Daddy's poll watchers, Gedney Howe, an old college friend, leaving the school yard. Mother raced down the steps and managed to intercept him. She could see that he was clearly upset, but he would tell her nothing. Returning to the school building, she learned that he had been threatened by a policeman brandishing brass knuckles, who told him to get home or his father, a city employee, would lose his job. By law, policemen were supposed to remain 100 feet from polling places, as Mayor Lockwood had so pointedly reminded my grandfather.

Furious, Mother decided to stay and watch that voting box herself.

After finding a ride home for the voter they had brought, Mother and Dorothy stationed themselves on the stairs overlooking the ballot box. Mother knew that she could stay there as long as she created no disturbance. She was determined to watch everything that was going on.

Someone recognized her and agreed to make a telephone call for her. "Please call my mother," she requested, "and tell her that Mendel's watcher has been kicked out and that I am guarding the boxes at Ward Twelve."

By the time the message reached my grandmother, it had become somewhat garbled: "Mendel has been knocked out at Ward Twelve and Margaret is standing over the body."

My grandmother hastily put on her best summer dress, her most becoming hat and her white gloves, and readied herself to depart. My grandfather attempted to reach his brother and friend Jack Maybank to ask them to go with him to Ward Twelve as a show of force.

Grandmother was so agitated that she could not wait for my grandfather to drive her to the polling place. She rushed out into the street, and, shedding all of her Victorian primness, hailed a stranger who was driving by and asked him to take her to Ward Twelve. Once there, she was calmed when she saw Mother, Dorothy *and* Daddy, quite unhurt, who had arrived there for a short visit on his rounds of the polling places.

My grandmother decided that she would see what was happening with the other ballot box in that ward. When the voting was completed, she followed the men in charge into one of the classrooms where they would count the votes. She was treated very rudely by some tough-looking men who tried to bully her and make her leave.

They didn't know my grandmother.

Henrietta Marion McCay Rivers, Mendel's mother, at about age 30.

Mendel, age six, with sisters Mildred, Madge and Blanche.

The house that Lucius Rivers built on the Bonneau Road in St. Stephen.

Mendel as a teenager.

Mendel's mother purchased this house on
O'Hear Avenue in North Charleston and
opened a boarding house.

Margaret Middleton and Mendel
Rivers, shortly after announcing
their engagement in 1938.

Mendel and his mother, 1938.

Mendel in 1938.

Congressman-elect Mendel Rivers, with his wife and daughter, Peg, shortly after winning the election in 1940.

John and Dot Neff with my father in Staunton, Virginia after the 1940 election.

The new Congressman
at work in 1941 in his
office in Washington.

Charleston Mayor "Tunker" Lockwood
strongly opposed my father's candidacy in
1940. Here, in 1941, he watches as
Congressman Rivers delivers a speech at
Stark Hospital. (Official War Dept. Photo,
Charleston Ordinance Depot).

Former political enemies, Congressman Rivers and Senator Burnet Maybank, being
interviewed by a newspaper reporter.

Two year old Peg with my mother at our house on Adams Mill Road in Washington, 1941.

Lottie, my parents' maid for many years, went to Washington with them after my father was elected to Congress.

Greenville, South Carolina Congressman Joe Bryson, with my parents in Washington, 1942.

Young Congressman Rivers speaking to the crew of the *U.S.S. Tidewater* during World War II. (Official U.S. Navy Photograph).

Herringstone, outside Staunton, Virginia, the farm my parents purchased in 1942.

Farmer Mendel Rivers.

My parents with my
sister Peg at Herringstone,
Christmas, 1946.

At Herringstone with
daughters Marion and
Peg, 1948.

Election Day, 1946, with his mother and
his wife.

Marion, Mendel, Jr., Margaret
and Peg Rivers in 1948.

Margaret Rivers, sponsor of the *U.S.S. Sirago*, at the launching in Portsmouth, N.H., in 1945. My mother said that she envisioned smashing the head of Adolf Hitler as she christened the ship with a bottle of champagne.

In August of 1947 my father sailed to Europe on Congressional business, pictured here with Gen. and Mrs. Omar Bradley, (front row center) and a group of teachers, bound for Germany.

In 1948, my father was quick to support the Presidential candidacy of Governor Strom Thurmond. Charleston pilot Beverly Howard (top right) flew my parents to Edgefield, Thurmond's home, Thurmond and wife Jean (left) greeted my father on his arrival.

My mother helping out in my father's Washington office, 1950.

My father frequently took family and friends to Citadel football games. Here, in the fall of 1951, neighbor Amelia Patat, daughter Marion and brother-in-law Harold Odom join him.

My father was an early fan of Billy Graham after hearing him speak in Washington. My parents introduce my sister Peg to Dr. Graham at one of his religious rallies in 1950.

Congressman Rivers and Speaker of
the House Sam Rayburn.

My father took me to New York for
my tenth birthday present in 1953.

After becoming a
Congressman, my father
enjoyed playing in the annual
Democrat-Republican
Congressional Game. He is
pictured here with Charleston
friend Harold Simmons.

My parents sailed to Europe in September of 1952. (U.S. Navy Photograph).

In our home in Charleston, 1952: Mendel, Mendel, Jr., Marion, Margaret, Peg and dog Maxie under sofa. (Photograph by Ronald Allen Reilly of Charleston)

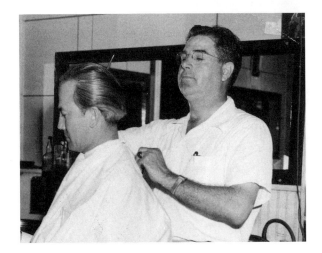

Known for his long hair, my father visits the barber.

In Washington in 1955, South Carolina Sen. Olin D. Johnston, Congressman
Mendel Rivers, Joseph P. Riley, Sr., and Sen. Strom Thurmond. (Courtesy of Mrs.
Joseph P. Riley, Sr.)

Congressmen Mendel Rivers and Frank Boykin (center) with Billy Graham.

"I have a right to be here," she told them. "Mr. Rivers says it's the law."

"I don't want no downtown women comin' up here to lean on me when I count the votes," said one surly individual.

"Oh, I can assure you that I have no intention of touching you," she replied primly and very properly. Some of the men snickered.

When the Chairman of the Charleston Democratic committee entered the room, he was most gracious to Grandmother, even getting her a chair. He assured her that if her personal tally didn't agree with that of the Administration watchers, that the whole box would be thrown out and recounted.

My grandfather and his brother Abbott arrived shortly thereafter in their best white suits, pistols at their belts. They stayed a short time, confident that the women of the family were in no danger.

Grandmother kept her vigil through the long process of counting. After a while a woman came in and whispered loudly, as she eyed Grandmother: "We've got to get her out of here. Rivers is leading in the counties by two thousand votes."

A disgruntled man responded: "Yeah, Rivers got his watchers after all. It's a dirty gyp."

In the end, however, Grandmother's tally matched with the official one, and while Daddy had not won in that ward, her presence had undoubtedly prevented an even more lopsided result.

Mother and Dorothy had followed another precious box of votes into a different classroom to be counted. They lined up by a wall and prepared to tally all the votes as they were counted out loud. Rivers' votes were mentioned only at long intervals.

One of Daddy's friends came up and spoke very softly to Mother: "See what they're doing? They've piled all of Mendel's votes on the bottom of that pile and he's flipping Mendel's votes off the bottom." Even though Mother saw how Daddy was being "counted out," she knew that she had to remain silent.

No one attempted to make her leave. However, the wife of a high-ranking Democratic official went up to her and snarled: "Why don't you get the hell out of here?"

"I have a perfect right to be here; it's the law," Mother calmly answered.

Glaring at her, the woman responded: "I'd like to spit in your eye."

They met again two weeks later, finding themselves standing next to each other on a street corner waiting for a light to change. On this occasion, the woman was gushing and all smiles: "Oh, hello, Margaret. I'm so glad to see you! We're having a party next week and you and Mendel *must* come." Mother declined politely. "Count us out *permanently*," she thought.

When the final tally was made, Mother asked one of the counters to verify her tally sheet, but he refused. Mother said that the man had once been a guest in her parents' home. His job and his livelihood in 1940 depended on his allegiance to the established power and he and his family had to eat. Mother said that they were both embarrassed and she wished she hadn't asked him.

With the exception of Daddy, Mother and her family were home by 10:30 that evening. Lottie Wright, their faithful maid, had remained with my infant sister Peg during their unexpectedly long absence.

Inundated with guests and telephone calls, they still weren't certain what the outcome of the election was. Seated in the large dining room, they hung over radio reports. Grandmother, hosting her first political victory party, provided tea and cookies for the visitors.

Finally, they heard Daddy's acceptance speech.

Joe Riley was with Daddy at the newspaper offices, then on Meeting Street, when the final count came in. So strong was the Democratic machine's voice in elections, that Daddy was hesitant about making any sort of acknowledgment of his victory until the final tally was verified by the Mayor. Joe and the *News and Courier* city editor, Tom Waring, guaranteed Daddy that the victory was his. Early returns from Charleston County were so heavily in favor of von Kolnitz that Daddy at one point considered conceding the election. He had lost Charleston County by 4,000 votes, but had won throughout the district by more than 3,000 votes. Once convinced of his success, he stepped up to the microphone in the small radio broadcast room of the newspaper office saying, "That's right! I don't have to listen to anything Lockwood says anymore."

The new Democratic nominee for the U.S. Congress spoke briefly: "You know I entered this campaign on my nerve and energy. I never had any money and haven't any now, but look how many friends I have. How am I going to thank all these good people? They know I appreciate it, I am sure...I would not feel that I had completed my campaign without expressing my heartfelt gratitude in the hour of triumph...As your representative in Congress, I shall always consider it my sacred obligation and duty to protect your interests and represent you to the fullest of my ability. We have won and our victory is complete."

Daddy arrived home at 2:30 a.m. He continued to rejoice with callers until nearly 4:30 when the well wishers had to practically be pushed out of the door. Congratulations began coming in again at 7:00 in the morning.

Daddy had won the election...and he had lost 17 pounds in the effort.

For days he was congratulated by countless people who went to his office to wish him well. One of them was Alfred von Kolnitz. A few years later, he graciously wrote Daddy a letter applauding his record of accomplishment in Congress.

Daddy lost no time in writing to the Chairman of the County Democratic Party, asking that the votes in four wards be recounted. The committee met three days after the election. The *News and Courier* described the meeting as the most bitter in ten years. Accusations of "fifth columnist" and "strong arm methods" were hurled back and forth. However, the committee resolved its differences and another protester decided to withdraw his own appeal. Daddy's request was denied.

Undaunted, he determined to take a protest to the South Carolina Democratic Committee. He drew up a strong, lengthy petition, indicating that the rights of all candidates, national and state, would be seriously affected if corrections were not made.

It was nearly impossible to have his petition served. Local officials suddenly became unavailable. The petition was finally served upon Mr. von Kolnitz who passed it on to county chairman, Mr. Sires.

A week after the election, Daddy and Mother drove up to Columbia, where the state committee met in the Capitol. Mother recalled: "I noted that Mayor Lockwood, a committee member, looked pale and drawn. It occurred to me that he was probably dreading public exposure of fraudulent practices. He needn't have worried; seasoned politicians were in charge of the meeting."

One committee member declared that Daddy's petition was "thoroughly out of order" because Daddy had already been declared the elected representative of the party.

Daddy retorted: "I've come here to ask you, for God's sake, to save the Democratic party. I am thinking solely in terms of those candidates who will run for office in the future. The greatest service any individual or group could render Charleston would be to clean up the rotten political conditions that exist in a few wards in that city." He declared that he had been denied managers in several precincts and that votes had been miscounted in several wards.

And, because he was the victor, not the loser, he added, "I'm probably the most unique protestant you've ever seen."

While several of the committee members voiced their approval of Daddy's request, they were greatly outnumbered. State Senator Edgar Brown, of Barnwell, said that it would be unwise to pursue Daddy's request, especially since the National Democratic party was facing a crucial situation: Wendell Wilkie, the Republican candidate for President, had stirred up a great deal of support in his radio addresses, and many Southern Democrats had decided to vote for him rather than for Roosevelt.

"Senator Brown was one of the smoothest of politicians," Mother remembered. "He made mollifying remarks about Mendel's being a fine young man. He mentioned that he was pleased to have served with Mendel in the State Legislature. He put his arm around Mendel's shoulder and declared his affection for such a capable young man.

"The Senator even said that he saw no reason to delve into Charleston's politics—'It was not the only place in South Carolina where there are political irregularities.'"

Daddy's complaint was ruled out of order on the grounds that he had already been declared the Democratic nominee and that statutory laws existed only to take care of election frauds.

The Mayor and the county Democratic chairman were interviewed by a newspaper reporter after their return to Charleston. The Mayor said that the action of the committee spoke for itself. Mr. Sires stated that Daddy's petition was just another attempt to smear Charleston's good name for political purposes.

Mendel Rivers, the underdog and the outsider, had fought and had won. And political hostilities generally abate after the final balloting is complete. My father got along quite well with those against whom he had competed during that campaign. As Congressman working for the First Congressional District, he was no longer the political enemy, but the friend.

CHAPTER 4

The new Congressman from the First District of South Carolina and his wife moved to Washington in February of 1941. They rented a row house on Adams Mill Road near Rock Creek Park.

Grandmama Shepard visited them shortly after they had gotten settled into their new home. She and Mother watched from the visitors' Gallery as Daddy took the oath of office at the swearing-in ceremony. Before taking his place on the floor of the House of Representatives for the first time, he looked up and searched through the many faces until he found theirs and waved a greeting; from then on, he always looked for his family and friends and waved to them. He and his mother later posed for a photograph in the Capitol's Hall of Fame beside the statue of Wade Hampton, for whom Daddy's father, Lucius Hampton Rivers, had been named.

At first, Daddy was assigned to the Merchant Marine and Fisheries Committee. Shortly thereafter in March, he was appointed to the Naval Affairs Committee, which would become part of the Armed Services Committee after the Congressional Reorganization Act following World War II. He had been interested, as well, in sitting on the Agriculture Committee as a means to better serve his largely agricultural state back home.

Another freshman Congressman was Edward Hébert of Louisiana, who would obtain a seat on the Naval Affairs Committee in 1943. He would succeed Daddy as Chairman of the Armed Services Committee in

1971. Daddy and Mr. Hébert became close friends and co-workers on the Committee over the years and shared similar convictions about U.S. defenses.

Miss Addie Huguenin, who had been the secretary for Tom and then Clara McMillan, continued to work for Daddy. He soon found that he needed a larger staff and hired Alex Boling, from Hampton, to come up and serve as his chief assistant. At that time, each Representative was allowed to hire three "clerks," and the total allowance for office staff was fixed by law at $6500 (no one clerk being permitted to earn more than $3900 per year). The allowance for stationery was $200 per session.

My father's salary was $10,000 a year. "I thought Mendel was being paid an enormous amount," Mother remembered. "I sometimes worried that someone would try to kidnap our precious baby for ransom because we were so rich."

Daddy plunged into the responsibilities and privileges of his office with his characteristic energy. With his outgoing manner and prodigious memory, he soon was on friendly terms with a great many of the members of the House and Senate.

One of Daddy's first friends in Congress was the ebullient Congressman from Mobile, Alabama, Frank Boykin—a truly unforgettable personality. He was a large man, always jovial and hospitable, who constantly declared his favorite saying, "Everything's made for love."

At the age of eight, Frank began his business career as a water boy for a construction gang for 35 cents a day. He soon doubled his wages by making himself a wooden shoulder yoke, so that he could carry two buckets instead of one. His energy and enterprising skill enabled him to amass several fortunes over the years.

His courtship of Occlo Gunn, the pretty, soft-spoken girl who would become his wife, began when he leapt from his horse onto a moving train. He saw her seated with three beaux and loudly announced, "I'm Frank Boykin and I'm going to marry you!" before he jumped from the train. She was not favorably impressed at the time.

He entertained lavishly both in Alabama and in Washington. Daddy sometimes joined the hunts for wild game that abounded on one of Frank's estates. Frank Boykin must have had a Midas touch: on one tract of land in Alabama, which he bought for a hunting preserve, was discovered one of the world's largest salt domes.

In 1941, Daddy and his colleagues found themselves facing increasingly threatening conditions against the United States and the free world. As a member of the suddenly critical Naval Affairs Committee, Daddy made many trips to inspect our country's fortifications, which all Americans hoped would not be tested.

He was also a member of the United States delegation sent to the British West Indies to talk to the British envoys regarding negotiations on the Lend-Lease program, which was playing a key role in Great Britain's defense system.

He told Mother that one of the British delegates approached him after one of the negotiating sessions and said in a stiff, formal and haughty manner, "I cawn't remember your name." Daddy calmly replied, "Well, just call me Mr. Lend-Lease. I am sure you can remember *that*, can't you?"

How exciting it was for Mother to be in Washington as the wife of a new Congressman!

Washington suffered during the Depression along with the rest of the nation, but conditions were quite different from those left behind in the South.

Daddy and Mother still had many debts and spent money cautiously. After she had been in Washington a few months, she wrote to her parents: "Everyone here spends so much on entertaining—always treating each other to food. I had a friend to lunch yesterday, and the tips, taxi, etc., came to $2.25, but can't be a cheapskate. It made me sick to see another friend shop and shop to save $2, then blow more than that on feeding another woman and me in a fancy place when they [she and her family] haven't even a telephone."

After going out for an evening with Florence, South Carolina Congressman, John McMillan and his wife Margaret, Mother said in a letter to her mother: "The John McMillans are very nice. We went out to dinner with them last night—the place was French, not fancy, but for 75 cents you get a wonderful dinner, and for 25 cents extra, all the wine you can drink."

Needless to say, the social whirl of Washington was vastly different from that of Charleston.

"Moving to Washington as the wife of a Congressman didn't terrify me, in spite of my natural reticence," Mother recalled. "Politics couldn't scare me—hadn't we weathered a campaign that broke the stranglehold of machine rule? As for society, hadn't I been a debutante in Charleston? I considered myself seasoned and somewhat sophisticated," she remembered, laughing at herself. "I had a lot to learn."

One of their early invitations was to attend a reception at the White House shortly after Franklin Roosevelt's third inauguration. They were greatly impressed by how gracious their hosts were as they received a mob of guests with warmth and cordiality. Because of the traffic snarls near the White House, they rode a street car from their home to attend it.

In those days, the wives of junior Congressmen were expected to pay calls on the wives of more senior and prominent people in Washington. Margaret McMillan, whose husband had served one term, took Mother under her wing to initiate her to the protocol ritual. Mother said that to her recollection they drove up the circular driveway to the White House portico and left their visiting cards for the President and First Lady without ever being asked for any identification.

Apart from the obligatory call at the White House, it would have taken super-human strength and dedication to pay all the other calls. In what was obviously a well-established custom, the wives of the different echelons of officials were expected to be at home on certain days to receive callers, with tea and refreshments laid out. One day was designated for the wives of the Justices of the Supreme Court, one for the Senators' wives, another for the wives of Representatives, one for diplomats' wives and yet another for the wives of high-ranking military officers.

One afternoon, dressed in fashionable finery, complete with saucy veiled hats, dangling fur pieces and spotless white gloves, Mother and Mrs. McMillan made the rounds of several embassies. They presented their cards, depositing them in the silver trays that the servants proffered. The corners of the visiting cards were properly folded to indicate that their husbands were not with them and that they weren't calling on the gentlemen.

Mrs. McMillan showed Mother how it was done. She delivered the correct query: "Is Madame in?" Although, on that afternoon, they were not admitted into any of the Mesdames' presences, they enjoyed getting a glimpse of the varying interiors of embassies, some of which, rather surprisingly, were far from grand.

When they stopped at a house near Dupont Circle, Mrs. McMillan suddenly whispered to Mother that it was her turn to speak. Flustered and thrown into confusion when a young man opened the door, Mother blurted out: "Is the madam in?"

Coldly eyeing the two women before him the young man said, "There isn't any madam here!" as he shut the door.

Mother admitted that once, while dressed in inelegant housecleaning attire, she was surprised by a visit from an exquisitely-dressed wife of a Congressman. Instead of pretending to be Mrs. Rivers' maid, she asked the lady in, who, clearly appalled, stayed approximately one minute before abruptly making her exit.

Mother enjoyed being in the 77th Club, which was composed of wives of the newly-elected members of the 77th Congress. She preferred that to the much larger group of all wives of Members of Congress, the Congressional Club, which held a tea every Friday afternoon. As the wife of a new Representative, she did, however, attend a luncheon at the Congressional Club early in 1941. She found herself standing in the buffet line behind Mrs. Everett Dirksen, wife of the (then) Republican Representative from Illinois. Mrs. Dirksen's companion asked her if she ever went to meetings of the 73rd Club (the Congress to which her husband had been elected). Mother was astonished when she overheard Mrs. Dirksen's reply: "No, I stopped going because there were so many Democrats there." Nurtured in the Solid Democratic South, she was amazed that all Democrats would be considered so objectionable.

Not too long after their arrival in Washington, they were invited to a large, formal dinner party. Cards indicated the names of their dinner partners. Daddy joined Mother shortly before dinner was announced, and she reminded him that he was supposed to find his dinner partner.

"I'll let him find me," Daddy replied. "For some reason, I'm supposed to go in with some Judge. I'll let him find me."

One of the other guests approached Daddy, saying, "The Judge is waiting for you; aren't you going to accompany her?"

Daddy quickly found Her Honor.

Social mores were vastly different from what we know today. Mother said that another Congressman's wife had called the hostess of that party to ask her permission to come "in her condition." She was expecting a baby and didn't want to embarrass anyone by appearing pregnant in mixed company. The hostess expressed doubt, but consented with reluctance.

Daddy was out of town when Mother answered the telephone one cold December afternoon in 1941. A friend of Daddy's, Nick Cureton, blurted out: "Have you heard the news? The Japanese have bombed Pearl Harbor! Turn on your radio! This means war!"

Daddy returned to Washington immediately for the emergency Joint Session of Congress. Roosevelt was in top form as he addressed the Congressmen and Senators, calling the day of the attack on Pearl Harbor a "day of infamy." Many Americans did not even know where Pearl Harbor was. The Congress was immediately galvanized into making a declaration of war.

There was one opposing vote against America's entry into the war—Jeannette Rankin of Wisconsin, the first woman ever elected to Congress. Ironically, she had also voted against the declaration of war by the United States during World War I. She was greatly affected by what was happening and rushed out of the House Chamber, unable to hide her tears. She locked herself inside a telephone booth to avoid answering reporters' questions. In the 1960s, still a confirmed pacifist, she participated in a peace march on Capitol Hill, protesting U.S. involvement in Vietnam.

The mode of living of Americans did not change immediately after the United States got into the war. Eventually, though, my parents and everyone else had to use black-out curtains and adapt themselves to rationing stamps and many scarcities such as gasoline, sugar, shoes and other items. The families of Congressmen were not exempt from the same privations that affected all U.S. citizens. Like the British, Americans learned to stand in long queues in stores, after obtaining a number to indicate their turn in line. Even baby diapers were confiscated to be used in munitions factories to wipe the grease from the machinery. Automobile factories were converted to manufacture weaponry. Americans learned to save tin cans and all other metal products that could be recycled into war materiel. With gasoline and tires scarce, neighbors shared rides for commuting to their jobs. Many people, Mother said, had to put their cars on blocks, for lack of tires, for the duration of the war. Mother said that decent shoes were especially hard to find; I still have scars on my chin where I cut it falling while clumsily learning to walk in poorly fitted shoes during the last years of the war.

Countless people suffered terribly because of the shortages in housing. Some military families often had to live in shanties and crudely-adapted structures for which they were forced to pay excessive rents. The situation became so desperate that rents were frozen.

Washington suddenly burst at the seams with the onset of the war. The population of the city doubled almost overnight. Rental property was particularly scarce.

When the year's lease was up on the house on Adams Mill Road, Daddy and Mother found a place in Fairfax Village, a housing development at the extreme end of Pennsylvania Avenue, Southeast, where a dozen or so other Congressional families lived. They felt lucky to be in small but newer accommodations, but, Mother said, the apartments were not particularly well designed or well managed. The lack of closet space made them determined to some day have ample storage space, an important feature which they included when they built a house in Charleston ten years later. When Daddy would bring home a bushel of apples or potatoes, as he was wont to do from time to time, they had to resort to putting the produce in the attic which was accessed through an opening in the small closet of my sister's room. Mother said that after I arrived in the spring of 1943, she couldn't get my baby carriage outdoors without removing the narrow kitchen table.

The apartment became less and less tolerable and the management took advantage of the tenants by overheating in the morning when the men were still at home, and gradually chilling the women and children during the day when the heat was off. On some days, frost formed on the insides of the window panes. Complaints were answered with the stock phrase: "Don't you know there's a war on?" A law suit finally forced the management to operate the complex more equitably, but, by that time, Daddy and Mother had moved again. A good friend of theirs, Alice Nager, persuaded an absent homeowner that they would make excellent tenants for her house on Glendale Avenue in Alexandria.

In the summer of 1942, my father authored a bill to have a 650-mile federally-operated oil pipeline built. The pipeline was designed to carry crude petroleum from the oil fields of Mississippi to the Southeast Coast to help cut the tremendous costs involved in transportation of this vital commodity for the war effort. The bill authorized an appropriation of $13 million for the pipeline, and was passed by both Houses of Congress, and signed into law by President Roosevelt.

For several months, the Petroleum Administrator, Secretary of the Interior Harold Ickes, did nothing to implement construction of the pipeline. There was opposition to the plan from large private oil firms, which were said to fear competition after the war to their established pipelines and refineries. It was the opinion of many that Secretary Ickes had bowed to the big oil interests and had steadfastly refused to proceed with the pipeline.

By February of 1943, still nothing had been done. Civilian gasoline rationing along the East Coast had become severe. Most transportation facilities available were being used in favor of bringing petroleum to Atlantic ports for shipment as part of the war effort. On the floor of the House, Daddy assailed Secretary Ickes: "The Secretary of the Interior says he does not think we need the line. Whose judgement is better, that of the Senate and House of Representatives, and of the President, or one man in the Interior Department?"

In March, Carl Vinson, Chairman of the House Naval Affairs Committee, appointed Daddy the head of a subcommittee to investigate the whole petroleum supply program. Members of the subcommittee held hearings in many parts of the country and met with the President in efforts to force the Interior Secretary to act on the pipeline legislation.

From the Hotel Adolphus in Dallas, Daddy wrote to Mother: "Thus far, our trip has been most gratifying. The testimony in Mississippi has convinced me—far beyond doubt—that not only is there sufficient oil for my pipeline, but amazing potentialities in future petroleum findings in that state. This is established by the fact that the big oil companies have spent millions in leases for oil since my bill passed Congress. I think my committee is really going to get out a scorching report."

The pipeline was never built. It was undoubtedly a frustrating experience for Daddy, but a valuable lesson in the ways of Washington—and of its powerful lobbyists.

Daddy found himself up against another strong interest group on Capitol Hill not long thereafter. In 1944, he introduced a bill to repeal the federal tax on colored oleomargarine. The dairy interests opposed him vigorously.

The dairy lobby had been influential in the passage of a federal law which placed a substantial tax on margarine if it was artificially colored to look like butter. Oleomargarine was considered an inferior substitute for butter, and uncolored margarine looked like nothing more than a block of lard. In an effort to make the product more appealing to the eye, the margarine manufacturer supplied a small amount of coloring matter in the packaging for the housewife to use to make it look like butter...and it was far more economical.

Daddy's bill met with strong opposition, particularly in the House Agriculture Committee. For several years, the bill, introduced time after time, simply "died" in the the committee. Daddy did not give up. He felt that, among other considerations, the cotton farmers deserved the right to be in competition with the dairy farmers—cotton seed oil was then often used in the manufacture of margarine. It was not even, ironically, a product which the farmers of Daddy's district in South Carolina produced.

Finally, after several years, Daddy circulated a petition for the required 218 signatures of Congressmen to force the Agriculture Committee to report the oleomargarine bill out of committee to the full

House for a vote. Wartime needs helped him in his efforts; it was becoming a national issue.

There were several rather heated and sometimes humorous debates on the floor during discussion of the bill. Daddy was often teased for saying in a speech that "the dairy industry is milking the housewives of America." The press latched onto it.

Daddy's long battle to repeal the tax earned him the name "Oleo Rivers." The legislation was finally passed in 1949.

We never used anything but oleomargarine at home. I was 15 years old before I tasted butter.

Daddy's Republican opponent, W. Tate Baggett, in the 1948 election, strongly suggested that Daddy had received a gift of $25,000 from the Cottonseed Crushers Association to sponsor the margarine bill. Daddy was furious and shot back a telegram which read: "In order that you might be properly classified, and for this purpose only, I am replying to your insolent, unfounded, unwarranted and malicious insinuations...I hereby and herewith state that any suggestion that I received anything other than my salary as a member of Congress from any source is unfounded in fact and false. The only basis to such a charge springs from your imagination and distorted brain."

It is ironic that today most margarine is made from soybean oil and its production benefits Midwestern farmers as much as it does Southern farmers.

For years he pushed for the use of oleomargarine rather than butter by the various branches of the military. In 1966, the Department of Defense ordered Air Force and Army installations to stop buying butter and to switch to less costly margarine, although the Navy was allowed to remain on the "butter standard."

Mother and Daddy felt especially blessed when their maid Lottie agreed to go and live with them in Washington after Daddy was elected. They paid her what was then considered generous, ten dollars a week, room and board and uniforms. They were very fond of Lottie and she was adaptable, capable and clever...and seemed to enjoy spoiling her employers.

Lottie had grown up in the country near Charleston and had worked previously for relatives of Mother. She once told Mother that her family had used oyster shells instead of knives and forks and that they had used their kerosene lamp only when company came to visit—otherwise, natural light or light from fireplace was their only source of illumination.

Lottie did the housework, was an excellent cook and took care of my sister. She never seemed to tire, Mother said, and did not complain of having too much to do.

After being in Washington for nearly a year, Lottie made her first visit back to Charleston. Mother and Lottie were driving around the Boulevard when Lottie suddenly commented: "I used to think Charleston was such a big town. Now, I think it's nuttinish."

Times were different and were changing, and so was Lottie. Her world in Washington was larger than it had been in Charleston, and, with the new exposure, she became increasingly dissatisfied with her employment with Mother and Daddy. She became very friendly with a white woman who must have belittled her domestic work and invited her into her home to use her bathtub and to wear her fur coat on her days off.

Mother was genuinely saddened that her relationship with Lottie eventually deteriorated beyond repair. Mother once found a discarded postal card addressed to a relative in South Carolina on which Lottie had written: "Mrs. Rivers is gettin too sicknin." After talking things over, they agreed that it would be best for Lottie to work elsewhere. After a while, they lost track of her but felt assured that Lottie's abilities probably served her well as she made a new life for herself.

Mother was further saddened, when, after Lottie had left her employ, she took my sister to the playground near their apartment where mothers congregated and watched their children play and quarrel. "Lottie in her uniform evidently had been the subject of conversation for the assembled white women. Many of these Northern women spoke pointedly about their dislike for Negroes. Lottie had often taken Peg there and she must have sensed their antipathy. I wish I had spared her that experience. She was a loving and friendly person and it hadn't occurred to me that the outings with Peg could have been such a trial for her," Mother recalled.

The war naturally increased the responsibilities and workload of Members of Congress and Daddy had to spend most of the time in Washington, but he was in Charleston whenever possible. Before the war, sessions of Congress had been brief, sometimes only a few months, but its sessions lasted the better part of the year during that continuous state of unrest. Since then it has become almost expected that Congress meet the entire year, sometimes ending on Christmas Eve.

Daddy moved his family back to Charleston for a time in 1944. As had been the case in Washington, rental units were in great demand and rents had been frozen by the government. We lived in a house that my grandmother Middleton owned on Queen Street.

Mother and Daddy found themselves living in a tall, four-story 18th-century row house whose charm, unfortunately, they discovered, could not mask its inconveniences. They had two jack-in plugs and one telephone which would invariably ring on a different floor. The government did not provide offices for Congressmen then, so the lovely drawing room became Daddy's office when constituents came to call. Mother said that she often had to accommodate the overflow of visitors at the dining room table, which sometimes had the unsightly remains of breakfast plates on it as she took care of her two small children and attempted to act as Daddy's receptionist as well.

Mother is convinced that living in that house made Daddy determine never again to live in one of Charleston's picturesque houses. She remembers his frustration when he, a gadget lover if there ever was one, enthusiastically purchased a special type of filter coffee machine. He had no success with it in either the kitchen or the dining room, and finally located a level surface in the drawing room where it would operate properly.

While living back in Charleston, tragedy struck Mother's family when her brother Charlie, a Marine Corps officer, was reported missing on maneuvers near Quantico on February 1, 1944. Mother and Daddy had attended his graduation ceremonies from Officers' Training School and had seen him a couple of times after that. For six weeks after the family had been notified that he was missing, no one knew if he was dead or alive. Daddy talked with several Marine Corps generals who were

71

extremely cooperative in trying to ascertain what had happened to Uncle Charlie, but to no avail. His body was found by a fisherman in the Chesapeake Bay. He left a two-year old son and his widow, Anne, who was expecting their second child.

It was an especially cruel blow to my grandmother who was making some progress in her recuperation from encephalitis contracted the summer before when the disease swept through Charleston, killing many. She was affected in walking, speaking and with double vision. She was so severely stricken that my grandfather felt compelled to have her declared *non compos mentis*. Early in her illness, she told me many years later, she had been able to hear her family around her talking about her imminent death, but had been unable to respond at all. Sheer determination to survive must have saved her. She eventually recovered completely and was able to resume her avid interest in historical research and writing. She ultimately published four books about early South Carolinians and was considered an authority on Jeremiah Theus, a Colonial painter, whose biography she wrote.

Early in 1945, my father took his family back to Washington when again their friend Alice Nager helped them to locate a house to rent—at 401 Fontaine Street in Alexandria.

In May of that year Daddy and Mother went to Portsmouth, New Hampshire, where she christened the new submarine *Sirago*. She said that she remembers her determination to break the champagne bottle on the first try: "I imagined the bottle to be Hitler's head."

They stopped over in New York on their way home. A friend of Mother's was able to procure theater tickets for them for every day of their visit. After a couple of performances, however, Daddy told Mother: "You'll have to find somebody else to go to all those plays. I'm going over to the Brooklyn Navy Yard to see the *Benjamin Franklin*." Understandably, he was much more interested in seeing the damaged aircraft carrier than in enjoying the theater.

The Navy Yard in Charleston became quite active during the war and there were times, of course, when there had been fear that Charleston would come under attack. During the early stages of the war, several of my parents' friends of German extraction were in open sympathy with Germany—even though some of them were third-generation Americans. Mother remembers having heard rumors about one German submarine that was captured off the coast of South Carolina during the war: when searched, butter wrapped in packaging from a local grocery store owned by German-Americans had been discovered.

Years later in Washington, Mother had lunch with several German women whose husbands were attaches in the German Embassy. It struck her at the time that it was a pleasant irony of life that after all the animosity of the war years that they could be sitting together making friendly conversation. She asked one of the women if she had ever been in Charleston. "No," she replied, "but my husband has. He was there once as a naval midshipman in 1927, and, then, of course, on the U-Boat in 1943."

Mother recalled fears, from time to time, that Germans would escape from one of the many prisoner-of-war camps scattered around the country, as was depicted in the popular wartime Oscar-winning movie *Mrs. Miniver*. There was a rather sad report in the newspaper once that told of the German prisoners in a camp in New England who thought they were being poisoned after being fed the typical white American bread because it was so unlike their dark German varieties.

Along with many other cities in the country, Charleston had a difficult time accommodating the sudden influx of military personnel. Many families with large homes were asked by the government, as part of the war effort, to house men and women in uniform. John Kennedy, as a young Naval officer, had a tour of duty in Charleston during the war, and, for a short time, lived in the home of my mother's Uncle Abbott Middleton. I do not know if Daddy and Kennedy ever had the opportunity to meet each other then but they did become friends after Kennedy's election to Congress in 1946.

The war finally ended.

Dick Bird, a commander on the *U. S. S. Missouri*, wrote to Daddy after the end of the Pacific war and described in poignant terms the Japanese surrender ceremonies on September 2nd on his ship: "The ceremony was topside on the superstructure deck and we had made no attempt to make things fancy. We even left the powder burns on the turret from our last bombardment of the Tokyo area...General MacArthur came on board last and then the Jap emissaries were called alongside and the little brown brothers came on board. Full honors were rendered everyone. The signing took only a short time and then the Japs departed, a defeated but strangely buoyant nation. A strange silence fell over the ship. This evening the sun sank over Fujiyama in one of the most beautiful sunsets I have ever seen. Slowly the lights of Tokyo came on— some of them for the first time in three years. I guess they feel safe now that our Fleet is in their backyard. Ironical, isn't it?"

Daddy departed in January, 1946, on an inspection trip to the Pacific, which originally had been scheduled for around the time of the bombing of Hiroshima. In preparation for this journey, he had to receive a lengthy and uncomfortable series of inoculations against dreaded and often deadly diseases—smallpox, typhoid, tetanus, yellow fever, typhus, cholera and plague. The group travelled some 18,000 miles and visited numerous military facilities to study the postwar feasibility of keeping certain bases intact and the tremendous logistical problem of disposing of surplus war material. In a little over three weeks, the delegation made more than 20 stops, many of them one night in duration. There was still much confusion in the area in clean-up endeavors, the resettlement of civilians and in efforts to bring the remaining American troops home. It would be a long time before the lush islands of the Pacific would be in any shape to beckon tourists.

During this trip, Daddy and his colleagues were briefed extensively about the ongoing war between the Communists and Nationalists to gain control in China. World War II had done little to abate those hostilities and the country continued to experience tragedy and devastation. From notes Daddy took on this trip, the U.S. Government had been aware for years of the assistance to the Chinese Communists from our recent ally, the Soviet Union. This, no doubt, did not come as a surprise to anyone. The U.S. had been an open and generous supporter of Nationalist Chiang Kai-shek, who, among other characteristics making him more acceptable to the West, was a Christian. In later years, Daddy became an ardent and vocal supporter of the Generalissimo and Madame Chiang.

One of the photographs that Daddy took in Tokyo presented a powerful statement about the mighty country that had attacked at Pearl Harbor a few years before; it was a picture of an automobile fueled by hay.

He went in August of 1947 as a member of another Congressional delegation to assess conditions in war-torn Europe and to help determine the role of the U.S. there. From aboard ship, crossing the Atlantic, he wrote to Mother: "The ship has many passengers—65 teachers—you should see and talk to them. For the most part, they are from the Mid West and Texas (Iowa, Missouri, etc.). They are enroute to Heidelberg to be sent over the occupied territory of Germany for instructing the children of the troops, the salary coming from the profits of the Officers Clubs. I'm not impressed with their knowledge.

"The remainder of the passenger list embraces Gen. and Mrs. [Omar] Bradley, a few other officers and their wives and goodly number of wives of officers and enlisted men. All of whom have howling, whining brats. I am flanked in my compartment by two such creatures. For the first three days I did little sleeping but now that it's cooler, I get a little more sleep.

"I addressed the group here Friday and gave them the works—had good reaction generally—some of the teachers objected to my favoring Universal Military Training—however, I don't expect school teachers—especially from the West, to have any conception of what this country faces. General Bradley observed he was surprised at this collective ignorance. I told him not to be because no one ever accused a teacher of having any common sense. When I return, I'll tell you what a delightful man he is and how fine Mrs. B. is.

"Last night we—the passengers—put on a variety show. I played the harmonica...The audience seemed to enjoy it. However, the star of the show was a Negress (holds a masters in music) enroute to join her soldier husband in Germany. She has composure, reserve—proud and possessed of a magnificent touch on the piano and a sweet, soft voice—her part was 'Indian Love Song' and 'Trees.'

"Be sure and contact the War Dept. if you need me or if the baby arrives before time...

"I have brushed up on my German a little and may be able to say a few words...I must start packing so I can leave tomorrow for Hamburg—thence to Berlin..."

Daddy remained friends with General Bradley. When, a few months after Daddy's death, the General spoke to the South Carolina State Chamber of Commerce, he paid my father a great tribute when he said that he had "scrapped" his prepared speech for the occasion when he had learned of Daddy's death. Recalling that he had first met the late Congressman "on a slow transport to Europe," he said, "The United States has not had a major war since World War II and I give Mendel Rivers great credit for the fact. The United States lost a tremendously strong voice for preparedness with Rivers' death...I lost a friend."

Daddy got home from that trip to Europe before the birth of his son, Lucius Mendel, Junior, who was born in Alexandria on October 6th. My father, like most men, was eager to have a son and namesake. (He had hoped that I would be a boy. Shortly before *my* birth in 1943, Joe Riley had sent him a check, for good luck,for $1, "For: Lucius Mendel Rivers, Jr.") When Daddy received word that he was finally the father of a son in 1947, he admitted later that he "went to bed a happy man."

In 1948, Daddy and six other members of the Armed Services Committee spent two weeks meeting with civilian and military officials in Germany, Austria, Italy, Greece, Spain and France. The belligerence of Russia had progressed to alarming stages and the U.S. was gravely concerned. It had become clear to the government of this country that participation in a military alliance with the countries of Western Europe was critical in order to check aggression from the east. "We are damn fools if we don't," Daddy told a reporter when asked if he favored the plan. He ardently supported the North Atlantic Treaty Organization (NATO), and served for many years as one of the Congressional delegates to the NATO Assembly.

He wrote Mother from Vienna: "Angel, by the time this arrives, Thanksgiving will have come and gone but I have been thankful for you, the kids and U.S. All that we've seen and heard has been of war and suffering. Then, too, the strain of what Russia may do to Europe...I almost forgot to tell you. We see *Madame Butterfly* tonight at the Opera. God, I wish you were here."

Daddy was appalled by how quickly the U.S. began to dismantle much of its defense network at the war's end. Budgets were drastically cut for the military and uniforms were happily shed as the nation hoped to settle into a hard-earned and lasting peace.

World War II had pushed the country into the position where she had to quickly shore up her own defenses and that of a large part of the world, as well. Daddy knew full well, as did many others, that Pearl Harbor would probably be the last time in our country's history when we would have the luxury of strengthening our defenses *after* being attacked. He was determined that the United States would never be in that position again. The war had catapulted America into a position of world leadership and economic superpower, and, like it or not, a great deal of this new role was tied to keeping our military strong and well-prepared.

Enemies had been defeated but enemies were still there and would continue to be. To be unprepared against the new Communist threats around the world would be no less than foolhardy, Daddy argued: "Trust Communists: Get along with Communism? Why, they've publicly avowed to bury us, and anyone who thinks we can get along with them is crazy." He consistently called on Congress never to allow America to let her guard down against this foe.

He was beginning to gain recognition then as one who took on many of the forgotten or ignored issues on behalf of those who had recently fought our battles, particularly the core of the military, those serving in the lower ranks. In 1946, he argued on the floor of the House of Representatives: "Today, the law of the land gives terminal leave pay to the officer personnel. Enlisted personnel is denied that provision of the law. This is a caste system, pure and simple, undeniable and undebated...There is a proposal to invest billions in foreign nations of the world [through foreign aid programs] by way of so-called loans without security. We, today, have an opportunity to invest in the men who saved our nation."

He never stopped thanking them for what they had done.

CHAPTER 5

One chilly day in the fall of 1942, Daddy received a call from John Neff in Staunton, Virginia, to tell him that a neighboring farm was up for sale. Daddy was delighted at the prospect and lost no time in driving with Mother to the Shenandoah Valley.

The Neffs drove them over to look at the property. When they drove up the narrow, rutted driveway, lined with bare maple trees, what they saw before them was a frame dwelling, with few architectural pretensions. Several haphazard structural additions had been made to the two-story Victorian house, apparently built around the turn of the century.

John Neff told them that the house was built by an Englishman, a Mr. Rawlinson, who married a local aristocrat, and had named it Herringstone after his home in England. His father in England had been a high-ranking, and apparently well-to-do, clergyman in the Anglican Church. Every time that Mr. Rawlinson received his allowance from his father, the story went, he jumped into his buggy and drove off to town to get materials to add on to his house.

As my parents explored the inside of the house, the results of Mr. Rawlinson's spontaneous renovations became painfully evident. Some of the interior doors, which were originally exterior doors, still held the heavy-duty, exterior hardware. The ceilings had different heights, resulting in several short staircases on the second level to connect the various room additions.

Daddy liked it immediately. Mother's impression was that the place was overwhelmingly dreary. Sensing her mood, he tried to encourage her: "It would be a perfect place for us in the summer, away from Charleston's heat and humidity, and we could easily come here for weekends and get away from the pressures of Washington."

She was uncomfortably pregnant again (with me) at the time and couldn't muster any enthusiasm. "Well, if you want it so much," she halfheartedly suggested to Daddy, "go ahead and put in a low offer, and see if it's accepted"—believing and hoping that the offer would be turned down.

It wasn't.

When Daddy returned from seeing the owner the next day, he was exuberant. "Congratulations, Marguerite! You're the new mistress of Herringstone."

For $5,000, he'd purchased 98 acres, the large dilapidated house, a run-down barn, fields and woodlands, unkempt lawns, a spring, several overgrown gardens and numerous neglected orchards. They had the first mortgage of their marriage.

The owner, Virginia Lotts, had inherited the property from the daughter of the builder. After nursing the older couple through long illnesses, she had remained to nurse their daughter, who died after a prolonged siege of cancer. The mother and daughter had been ardent horticulturists and had taken many trips to visit gardens around the world. That they had not been interested in interior decoration and design was obvious to my mother.

It didn't take her long to realize why their ridiculously low offer on the farm had been accepted with such alacrity. There was an air of gloom about the place. Fresh coats of paint and new wallpaper didn't seem to help, as Mother had hoped. At times, she was convinced that the house was haunted: "Twice I heard someone run his hand along the piano keyboard. I also heard, or thought I heard, my name called several times when no one else was around."

She wasn't alone in her reactions. Several visitors remarked to her on how spooky the house was. My parents once offered the use of Herringstone to a member of Daddy's Washington staff for her honeymoon. A long time later she told Mother that she and her bridegroom had been so uneasy at Herringstone that they had left it on their wedding night and had gone to a hotel. Even Daddy confessed years later that he didn't like being there alone, and on two different occasions had left it for the security of a hotel in Staunton.

At first, the rats in the attic were particularly alarming. They could hear them scampering overhead in what Daddy called the Rathill Downs. They were eventually eradicated.

Daddy loved his farm. He would cheerfully shovel snow, keep the coal furnace going, make fires and help cook over the old wood-burning stove. He enjoyed calling the Neffs on the old-fashioned telephone on the wall, which operated by ringing the numbers with a revolving crank handle. Eventually, two new bathrooms were put in and the old one improved. Daddy installed modern telephones with several extensions, and even managed to get a washing machine, a wartime luxury. In time, my parents extended the kitchen and added a breakfast room that had a lovely view of the three mountains in the distance, the names of which delighted us as children: Betsy Bell, Mary Gray and Little Molly Cottontail.

It did not take Daddy long to have the old orchards cleared and to replant sixteen acres of fine apple trees and eight acres of peaches. Alone, he planted a large vegetable garden behind the house, which could have fed a small community. Some of the old trees produced plums and crabapples, and Mother was soon mastering the making of jellies and preserves.

They tried numerous times to get someone to help with the housework and the children but were unsuccessful. Mother could understand why the help they had in Charleston did not want to stay at Herringstone with no companionship or diversions. The farm was nine miles out of town in an area known locally as "Stingy Hollow." One morning Mother was annoyed to hear someone blowing the horn of his car continuously in front of the house. When she opened the door, the rural mail carrier announced:

"Well, here's your chickens. Please sign here for them."

"Chickens! There's some mistake. I didn't order any chickens!"

"It's got your name on them. I'll put them on the porch for you."

Daddy had ordered two hundred milkfed, double-breasted baby chicks—without mentioning it to Mother!

With the help of a kindly old black man, who occasionally helped with some of the farm chores, Mother flattened out tin cans to nail over the rat holes in the old back kitchen and tacked chicken wire over the doorway. The Neffs lent a brooder, which they installed. The chicks were soft, fluffy things and, as much as Mother didn't want them, she knew she couldn't let them die of neglect.

When Daddy arrived shortly thereafter, he complimented Mother on having housed the chicks so successfully. "I knew you'd like them when you saw them."

Daddy built a permanent home for the young chicks next to the pen where he housed two young pigs. He expected to market the eggs at the farmers' cooperative, which, of course, he had joined years before. His mother had raised chickens and sheep and Daddy could not understand why his wife couldn't muster up the same enthusiasm for the farm.

After about five years, Daddy made arrangements to sponsor DPs (Displaced Persons), refugees from war-torn Europe, to come and work at Herringstone. He engaged a family from Latvia who had survived the horror of war, having been forced to work in a German munitions factory after escaping the Russian armies who overran their tiny, helpless country.

Anton and Herta Zvirgdins spoke no English, but Daddy knew enough German to communicate with them. Their teenage daughter, Valda, had contracted tuberculosis and Daddy arranged for her to be hospitalized in nearby Charlottesville where she was cured after a long stay.

Daddy went to Staunton to help them become situated in their new environment. He was thrilled to see how hard they worked and jubilantly described to Mother how they had removed every bureau drawer, cleaning every surface inside and out, and rearranging the contents in perfect order.

When Mother met them a few months later, she was both amazed and appalled to see just how hard they had worked to tidy the house and grounds. Scattered pins in a dish had been meticulously arranged in a circle with all the points in the center. Spice cans had been scrubbed and polished and arranged in a zig-zag pattern on the shelf. To Mother's horror, Anton, in his zeal for orderliness, had cut down the hedge enclosing the little side garden that she enjoyed cultivating. Now, the only thing between her garden and a cow pasture was an unsightly barbed wire fence. At that time, my brother Mendel was a toddler who didn't want any part of Herta, nor she of him. Instead of becoming the hoped-for helping nurse, she'd follow Mother and Mendel around with a woe-begone expression and tidy up any disorder that the child had created.

Once Mother heard thumping in the kitchen in the middle of the night. When she went downstairs to investigate, she discovered Herta in tears on a ladder, washing the kitchen walls. By then, Herta knew a little English, but communication was still difficult. Mother told her as gently as she could:

"Herta, you don't have to do that. You ought to be in bed."

Undaunted, Herta replied, "No, Meeses, in Latvia, we like putty."

"I like pretty, too, Herta, but you need your rest." Mother said she resisted the temptation to tell her that she, too, needed her rest.

Another time she found Herta crying over the ironing board at six in the morning, ironing the children's socks and panties.

"Herta, what's the matter?"

"Too much works, Meeses, too much works."

"But you don't have to iron these things," Mother pointed out.

"In Latvia, we like putty," she replied through her tears.

Daddy was so encouraged by the thorough and competent help that one summer he and Anton planted *13 acres* of tomatoes, one of Daddy's favorite foods. He had planned to sell what the family could not use to the local markets, but, unfortunately, when they ripened, he was overseas on Congressional business. Anton harvested a super abundance and Herta spent days canning the fruit while Mother searched about for ways to give it away. Anton and Herta became so distressed that much of the crop would go bad that Mother finally loaded up her car with bushels of tomatoes and took them to a local grocer who bought them from her for $4 a bushel, a ridiculously low price. The grocer then sold the tomatoes for 25 cents a pound, a high price even then. Mother gave her profit to Anton and Herta. When Daddy finally returned, he congratulated everyone for the fine job they had done with the tomato harvest—especially Herta who had canned more than 200 quarts of tomatoes.

Anton and Herta were especially pleased with the little chickens and took great pride in caring for them. The chicks were only about half-grown, however, when some of them began to keel over and die. Herta was distressed, and Mother not so much, but the county agent was called to come and diagnose their ailment.

The agent examined the deceased chickens and told Mother that they were being fed laying mash prematurely. He said that they would be all right if they were weaned off of the laying mash gradually and put back on the regular mash until they were more mature.

It seemed simple enough. Mother began explaining what to do in elementary English and gestures to Anton and Herta, pantomiming laying mash and regular mash. The longer she talked the more the Latvians eyed her with growing hostility.

"What's the matter?" Mother asked. "Do you understand what I am saying?"

Greatly offended, Herta responded grimly: "Meeses, we goot. We no eat chicken food."

Once Mother arrived at Herringstone and was greeted by a frantic Herta who ran out of the house, waving a postcard in her hand. The card was a routine notice from the Immigration Service reminding the Zvirgdins family of their regularly-scheduled registration visit which needed to be made during the current month. Herta was distraught and wanted to leave immediately to drive into Staunton. Having just made a four-hour trip from Washington with three fussy children, Mother told her that she would take her later. Herta, Mother recalled, was sullen for hours. After her many terrifying experiences during the war, Herta considered anything from government authorities as something that had to be acted upon at once.

It took more than a year for Mother and Herta to become friends, but once they did, they were devoted to each other.

When my parents sold Herringstone in 1951, Daddy found employment for Anton in Michigan for much higher wages than he had been able to pay him. Anton and Herta refused to leave for the new job until the packing and moving chores had been completed. Anton built sturdy wooden boxes into which he and Herta carefully packed all the goods for moving. They gave us their little dog Maxie who was the best of a litter born under the breakfast room; they had taught him to wipe his feet on doormats. The parting with Anton and Herta was filled with hugs and tears.

Herringstone was sold to a retired Naval officer for $20,000—their only offer—after having had it on the market for over a year. Daddy figured that he had just about broken even.

CHAPTER 6

Shortly after the election of 1950, Daddy telephoned my mother from Charleston and proudly announced: "Marguerite, I know how much you've always wanted to have a house of old Charleston brick. Well, I just bought the bricks, so get your plans together so that we can start building."

He was immensely pleased that he had been able to acquire the fine old brick from the recently razed "Ryan's Jail," a large building that had stood on the south side of Queen Street. The structure, a former detention center, had been across the street from No. 24 Queen Street where our family had lived for nearly a year during World War II.

Mother, who was nursing three sick children at the time, felt that the last thing she could do was to decide on a house plan. When she protested, Daddy, typically a man of action, said that he would tell the contractor what to build if she didn't get some architectural plans to him soon. Naturally, she got to work quickly. She recalls scanning magazines for house ideas and going to a local drugstore to buy house plans which were then sold for the mass market in those boom days of house construction after the war.

Part of Daddy's urgency to get the house built stemmed as much from his temperament as from America's growing involvement in the hostilities in Korea. He was fearful that building materials would become unavailable as they had during World War II.

Daddy and Mother had often talked about the possibility of building or buying a permanent home in Charleston. They had recently purchased a lot in Wappoo Heights, a suburb across the Ashley River outside of the city, next to Daddy's good friend, Leon Patat. Mother was reluctant to make the commitment. The house they were currently renting in Alexandria was comfortable enough, and they had lived in it for three years, longer than they had ever lived in one home since they had married. She was not anxious to uproot her children, as she felt we were happy and well-adjusted where we were.

The construction began early in 1951.

It took nearly a year to complete the house at 9 Palmetto Road. "I was often frantic over some of the things Mendel wanted to do in the house," Mother remembered. "He purchased some lovely cypress paneling, quite popular at the time, and intended to panel *every* room in the house. I rescued only two bedrooms, the living room and the entrance hall."

Probably the most outstanding room in the house and the one of which Daddy was the most proud was his 13 by 22 foot kitchen. For the early 1950s, it was considered quite spacious and modern. Daddy loved to cook and to have every up-to-date appliance and gadget available to him, oftentimes in multiples. Perfectionist that he was, he could get quite irritable with any of us when discovered using the wrong knife for a particular chore, or, worse, not replacing a utensil in its proper place.

He thoroughly enjoyed his kitchen and, since he was up hours before the rest of the family, he usually had the coffee brewed, orange juice squeezed and a pot of grits on the stove by the time the rest of us appeared. He particularly liked to entertain in his kitchen, especially early in the morning, and frequently invited friends and colleagues visiting Charleston to join him for breakfast at 7 a.m.

And one thing the house does have is ample storage space, a feature Mother and Daddy had lacked in all other homes where they had lived.

Mother moved down from Washington after the close of the school year in the summer of 1951. That summer we lived in four temporary places, including two different beach houses, my grandparents' house on New Street and a motel. We moved into the new house in October.

And brand new it was. The floor finishers put down strips of brown paper on the newly-finished wood and literally backed out of the front door as the movers brought furniture in the back door. Most electrical sockets did not have plates to cover them. Sawdust seemed to be everywhere. I remember running in terror to Mother one day, screaming that I had seen a "Tarantula;" what I had seen was a sawdust-covered cockroach.

Workmen were still putting on numerous final touches all over the house when Mother and Daddy had their first houseguests, General and Mrs. Harry Collins, who came down from Columbia where he was the commanding officer at Ft. Jackson. They walked over the new brick pathway that had just been laid. When they got into their room, Mother had to ask that they allow a man to come in to complete the installation of the Venetian blinds at the windows.

General Collins had been the occupation commander in Salzburg after the close of World War II where he had met his lovely Austrian wife, Irene. Harry Collins is buried in an ancient churchyard in Salzburg, a special concession which was allowed by grateful citizens who wished to show tribute for the Americans' just treatment of them after the war.

Mother recalls those early years at 9 Palmetto Road as endless days of chauffeuring her three children to their various activities. I always thought we lived practically out in the country although we were only five minutes from downtown Charleston. Before my sister and I began driving, we complained constantly that we lived too far from everything important. After we got our driver's licenses, Daddy gave us the first Volkswagen Beetle to appear in Charleston—a novel little car then and one that got us a lot of attention.

It was not too many years before the area began changing from quiet suburbia to a rapidly-growing section full of commuters. Traffic going to and from the many new sprawling developments beyond our neighborhood began to annoy Daddy. The longer he had to wait before getting onto the two-lane highway near our home, the more irked he would get. In 1955, he prevailed upon the Highway Department to install a traffic light at the intersection. Plans were in the making for widening this section of highway, and the traffic was becoming as much of a danger as an annoyance.

"Please tell my dear friend Claude McMillan [the Highway Commissioner] how vital the traffic light is to us at Wappoo Heights," he wrote to Julian LeaMond in the Legislature. "This is my #1 Project because I love my children..."

The light was eventually installed and became known to many as "Mendel Rivers' Light."

Both Daddy and Mother enjoyed gardening and welcomed the challenge to cultivate the large expanse around their house. They put in untold hours of effort to create what is a lovely garden full of azaleas and camellias—Daddy prided himself in knowing the Latin names for all of his plants.

It is impossible to think of that yard without thinking of Thaddeus, the black yard man who worked for my parents for over 20 years. Daddy and Thaddeus had instant rapport from the first day that Thaddeus, with an almost constant smile on his face, appeared at our back door. Daddy's good-natured teasing, ability to direct and his use of strong language endeared him to Thaddeus immediately, who knew instinctively how to get along with "duh Boss." He would often break into laughter when Daddy would correct him. Thaddeus genuinely loved gardening and did his best to please Daddy...which was not always easy.

Mother, on the other hand, had to supervise Thaddeus during Daddy's frequent absences, and took longer to accept him. She often felt that he sometimes used clever subterfuges to avoid work and seemed to move in slow motion. To make matters worse, he was very hard of hearing (and never got used to wearing the hearing aid that Daddy and his other neighborhood employers gave to him).

Whenever Mother came into sight, however, Thaddeus would remove his hat and, with a gallant sweep of his arm, bow from the waist, making her feel like a grand duchess. Once, when she was certain that he was carefully trying to get out of doing some chore, she found him kneeling in prayer, and she was certain that he was praying to be able to get along with the wife of "duh Boss." After that, they got along much better.

One time when Mother complained to Daddy about Thaddeus, he

tried to soothe her by saying, "Oh, Marguerite, he's a good man. *I* can get lots of work out of him."

"Well, I can't," Mother replied, "and I'm going to have to take tranquilizers if you keep him around here."

"Then get yourself a bunch of them, darling, because Thaddeus stays."

Thaddeus was a member of a vanishing generation of Southern blacks—reared on a large plantation around the turn of century and largely uneducated. He spoke in the rich Gullah dialect, peculiar to the coastal areas of South Carolina, and almost incomprehensible to people from other parts of the country. But Thaddeus capitalized on his strengths—knowing, possibly sensing, that his congeniality and gift of laughter were his most valuable assets for getting along in an increasingly complex world. His unique and lovable charm endeared him to our family and had undoubtedly carried him through many difficult times.

Thaddeus had a special affinity for children and animals. He could cajole barking dogs and crying babies into serenity. When my nephew Robert was about two years old, he found that one of the greatest delights in visiting his grandparents was to be around Thaddeus. Once, Robert was dawdling over his meal when Thaddeus came into the kitchen. The toddler immediately proffered some of the food to Thaddeus who grinned from ear to ear, bowed low, shook Robert's hand and then kissed it. Robert went all over the kitchen giving Thaddeus everything in sight and each time Thaddeus thanked him profusely. From then on, Robert wanted to have all of his meals with Thaddeus.

It was my parents' accepted routine to provide three full meals for Thaddeus on the day that he worked at the house. Usually, Mother would prepare a tray of food that Thaddeus would, by preference, eat on a porch overlooking the yard. As Mother would hand him the tray, he would say: "Thanks the Lord!" Then, almost as an afterthought, he'd add: "And thanks you, too, Miz Rivers."

Any guests in our home who had the opportunity to meet Thaddeus were usually delighted by his friendly nature, but one who resisted his charms was Admiral Hyman Rickover. While he, Daddy and Mother were enjoying coffee one morning, Thaddeus appeared in the living room to ask something of Daddy. When the Admiral did not reply to his polite greetings, Thaddeus became effusive. Admiral Rickover was well known for his silent treatment of unfavored individuals and this became increasingly evident as he watched Thaddeus do everything he could to get a favorable response. Thaddeus bowed deeply in front of the guest, then finally grabbed Admiral Rickover's hand and kissed it. The Admiral simply stared at him.

Once, after a severe rainstorm, Thaddeus came in a couple of hours late. Daddy, eating at the kitchen table, winked at Mother, and in a loud voice said: "Well, Thaddeus, I know you're here for your money. What do you expect me to pay you now, getting here so late?"

"I don' expec' nuttin', Boss. I don' work fuh duh money. I come here becuz I know Miz Rivers need me to come here to help. I don' want you to give me nuttin', Mistuh Rivers. No, Suh!" Then Thaddeus ambled outside into the yard.

Daddy looked at Mother sheepishly. "Well, he really took the wind out of my sails!" Daddy deducted nothing from the check he gave Thaddeus as he left early.

Daddy truly enjoyed Thaddeus. Kathy Worthington, a member of Daddy's office staff, recalled an occasion when she took some important papers and messages to our home in Charleston that required his attention. She said that dozens of people were trying to reach the Congressman and the office was swamped with visitors and telephone calls. When she arrived at the house, she found Daddy sitting in front of the television set watching a football game and eating fried chicken. Nearby, Thaddeus sat respectfully enjoying the chicken, the game and the company of "duh Boss."

When Daddy was in the hospital in Birmingham for heart surgery, Amelia Patat, our next door neighbor, sent Daddy a note which Thaddeus had dictated to her:

Dear Mr. Rivers,

I send you good prayers. Every day I
prays for you. I trying to take care of
everything until you reach home. I misses
the cigars you give me. I will finish

90

planting the bulbs. Let me know when you
coming home. Hope you will be here for
Christmas. I misses you so much.

Thaddeus

Amelia added that Thaddeus said to her: "Mr. Rivers is going to have to stop his cussing and start praying. Every time he opens his mouth, a cuss word comes out."

After Daddy died, Thaddeus made it clear to my mother that he would not approve should she consider marrying again. Thaddeus once asked Mother: "Miz Rivers, my boss been a big shot, ainty?"

"Yes, Thaddeus, he was a big shot."

"Well, Miz Rivers, I ain' gonna git no mo sweet big boss and you ain' gonna git no mo big shot husband. Miz Rivers, don' you bring no mo boss around here, cause if you do, I ain' gonna do *nuttin'* he tell me!"

Thaddeus died at the age of 72 in 1976.

CHAPTER 7

"President Truman is a dead bird," Mendel Rivers declared during a speech on the Floor of the U.S. House of Representatives.

My father found himself at odds with his own political party many times throughout his political career, and he certainly didn't hesitate to say so. Indeed, he had begun his career that way. That his seat came to be considered one of the most secure in Congress attests to the fact that his constituents must have liked the outspoken Mendel Rivers they returned to Congress every two years.

In 1948, tensions within the Democrat Party reached explosive levels, and Daddy became an active and vocal critic of the national Democratic Party. His "dead bird" remark made national headlines.

Many people in the country voiced concern over the gradual encroachment by the federal government into private lives and local affairs, a situation which had accelerated during the Depression years with the massive amount of emergency federal legislation that had been enacted. Daddy was among those who felt that the very essence of this country's strength lay in having distinct and autonomous levels of government and he saw this strength being severely eroded. A lot of Southerners agreed with Governor Earl Warren of California who called for "decentralization of authority because the strength of the republic depends largely on the virility of the state and local governments." An odd bedfellow indeed, Warren quickly became an enemy to many whites in the South after the enforced integration of Little Rock schools a few years later when he was Chief Justice of the U.S. Supreme Court.

There were many points of contention within the Democratic Party nationwide, but the main issue in 1948 was the Party's call for a federal mandate to force the inclusion of blacks, largely concentrated in the South, into the voting ranks of the Party. While much has changed since then, in 1948, many cynics, perhaps nearing the truth, viewed the voting rights issue as a means of winning elections rather than for any lofty Constitutional principles. When, in the 1950s, the Republicans introduced controversial pieces of civil rights legislation, they were accused of the same thing.

At the Democratic National Convention in Philadelphia in the summer of that year, emotions became so heated that Southern delegates were booed and jeered. The entire Mississippi delegation and some of the Alabama representatives walked out.

The aftermath of the convention resulted in the formation of the States Rights Democrats or Dixiecrat Party. In Birmingham, Alabama, the Dixiecrats held their own convention and nominated South Carolina Governor Strom Thurmond as their presidential candidate, with Governor Fielding Wright of Mississippi as his running mate. Few thought that Thurmond could win the election, but the Dixiecrat protest aimed to show the national Democratic party that a Southern bloc possessed enough clout to possibly influence the outcome of the election.

Strom Thurmond, then in his forties, had already served as a lawyer, teacher, state senator, Army officer during World War II and circuit judge before becoming governor, elected over a field of ten other candidates. He was immensely popular and considered progressive in the field of education.

His personal life had attracted national attention the year before when he had married a former "Miss South Carolina," Jean Crouch. She had gone to work for the Governor as his secretary shortly after her graduation from college and he had proposed marriage in a letter he dictated to her. The day before the wedding, he posed for a *Life* magazine photographer by standing on his head to prove that he was youthful enough to marry someone 23 years his junior.

Daddy actively supported the Dixiecrat movement. He and Thurmond had known each other since the 1930s when they had served together in the State Legislature. "Mendel came out strongly right away for the States' Rights movement," Senator Thurmond told me. "It was more a movement than a party and he didn't wait to declare himself. If anyone knew Mendel Rivers, they knew that there wasn't any middle ground. He was for or against. I've always appreciated his support in 1948."

On election day, Daddy and Mother flew to the Governor's hometown of Edgefield and accompanied the Thurmonds to the polling place when the candidate cast his vote.

Strom Thurmond received 39 votes in the Electoral College, enough to gain notice, but not enough to deadlock the election. The most far-reaching result of the 1948 schism in the Democratic Party for the South, though, was that one-party politics came to an abrupt end.

Daddy's support for the Dixiecrats could have seriously affected his seniority and position in Congress, but it did not. Apparently, no one was severely punished for supporting Thurmond over Truman. It, no doubt, had been a painful enough experience for the Democratic Party without making it worse after election day when unity in Congress was important.

It was certainly not the last time that Daddy would express his disagreement with the national Democratic Party.

Blacks in the South did gain a highly-publicized entry into the voting ranks of the Democratic Party. And, in 1950, Mendel Rivers was opposed for re-election in the Democratic primary by the first black to run for federal office in the South since the bitter Reconstruction days following the Civil War.

Arthur Clement, his opponent, was heavily backed by the NAACP, but, from what I have been told, the campaign never became embroiled in heated racial overtones. The fact that a black would run for Congress in the South at that time was astonishing to most whites, and to a great many blacks, as well.

Daddy was confident that his ten years in Congress amounted to something with the voters. He won the election by a large margin, receiving nearly 45,000 votes to Clement's 7,000.

My father got along fairly well with his black constituency. In later years he worked hard to get federal funding for job training, day care centers and other programs to assist the blacks economically in his district. Blacks outnumbered whites in much of Daddy's district, but he always received an overwhelming majority of the black vote even when he had a black opponent.

Daddy was admittedly a segregationist and was, of course, a product of his generation and environment. He later broadened the sometimes narrow point of view held by many Southerners and Northerners alike regarding the status of blacks. Many people in the South feel that our close dealings with blacks have probably made legislated integration efforts go much more smoothly than in some other parts of the country where no prior relationships existed. Some blacks who moved "up North" have returned, finding conditions for them outside of the South far less desirable than they had thought they would be.

There were times, I think, when my father rather enjoyed his little rifts with Truman.

Early in 1951, columnist Drew Pearson, ever eager to be on the inside of the Capital's gossip, reported in his "Washington Merry-Go-Round" column: "It's news when a Dixiecrat gets invited to the White House, particularly a dyed-in-the-cotton Dixiecrat like Representative Mendel Rivers of South Carolina, who figured prominently in the revolt against President Truman in the 1948 election.

"However, Truman rolled out the welcome mat for the silver-maned South Carolinian the other day as though he were a long-separated fraternity brother. The reason is that the President wanted Rivers' support for the 18-year old draft bill. After a brief reference to the legislation, the two antagonists spent the rest of the meeting assuring each other that there were no 'hard feelings' between them.

"'If you are a big enough man to invite me down here, I'm big enough to accept the invitation, Mr. President. In fact, it's a pleasure to accept,' grinned Rivers.

"'Some people have been saying that I don't like you and would never invite you down here, Mendel,' responded Truman. 'Well, it isn't so. I've never closed the door to you. I want you to know that it will be open any time you want to see me.'"

A visit to the White House did not, however, improve their philosophical and political relationships. Daddy criticized "Truman and his crowd" for their attempts, as he saw it, to destroy certain fundamentals of the Constitution. The Executive Branch, he felt, was blatantly usurping power—exemplified by the seizure of the striking steel mills in 1952 (a month later declared illegal by the Supreme Court), advocation of socialized farms and medicine, and the support of various pieces of labor legislation.

Worst of all, perhaps, was the Chief Executive's handling of foreign affairs.

A great admirer of General Douglas MacArthur, Daddy was alarmed when Truman fired him as supreme commander in the Far East in 1951. While admitting that MacArthur had disobeyed orders, prompting the dismissal, Daddy felt that Truman had made a "grave mistake."

The "deposed far eastern commander," as Daddy once called MacArthur, spoke to Congress after his return to the United States. Daddy had several television sets put in both his office and home so that visiting constituents and friends could watch the address. That day the House Visitors Gallery was filled to capacity with spectators wanting to see and hear the famous General. The speech he gave became known for the line, "...old soldiers never die, they just fade away."

For 11 years MacArthur officially was an officer who had been removed from all command for alleged insubordination. Daddy remained one of MacArthur's strongest supporters in Congress. It was not until 1962, though, that Congress agreed to adopt a joint resolution, sponsored by Daddy and approved unanimously by both Houses of Congress, which changed the way history would forever view the controversial General.

On that occasion, during ceremonies on the steps of the Capitol (to accommodate the large crowds), Daddy called MacArthur "the greatest soldier of our time" before the General was presented with the resolution which expressed "the thanks and appreciation of the Congress and the American people...in recognition of his outstanding devotion to the American people, his brilliant leadership during and following World War II..."

Early in 1952, Daddy expressed a brief interest in seeking the federal judgeship position for eastern South Carolina, a position which would, of course, have required the blessing of none other than President Harry Truman.

Daddy had been urged to run for the federal bench to fill a vacancy created by retiring Judge J. Waites Waring, the man who had handed down the decision to include blacks in the voting ranks of the Democratic Party a few years before. Waring, a member of a prominent Charleston family, had become quite controversial both judicially and socially in Charleston, having entertained blacks in his home. Many local residents were upset with his behavior, and a cross had even been burned the yard of his home in downtown Charleston.

Daddy had been highly critical of him and had even spoken out for his impeachment. He ultimately succumbed to pressure from friends and constituents to remain in Congress. In withdrawing his name from consideration for the seat, Daddy said: "Were I to become a Federal judge, I would be barred from entirely free expression. I would be most unhappy to find myself in such a position." Unhappy indeed.

More than likely, Truman would not have nominated Daddy. In the end, Ashton Williams of Lake City was nominated by the President for the appointment. Williams had been the leader of the pro-Truman movement in South Carolina in 1948 while Daddy had been supporting the Dixiecrat movement and calling Truman a "dead bird."

Daddy hoped, having served as a delegate to the Democratic National Convention in Chicago in 1952, that Adlai Stevenson would seek to mend the wounds that had festered within the Party since the 1948 election. But a few months later, he publicly repudiated Stevenson, in a radio address, for being a mouthpiece for Truman:

"When I left the Chicago Democratic convention, I hoped that Governor Stevenson meant what he had been saying. I was prepared to support his candidacy in the belief his election would mean a change, a new outlook, new faces, new politics, supplanting Trumanism by a return to traditional Democratic principles and beliefs. I thought Stevenson meant it when he wrote of his belief in states rights. I thought the time had come when the Democratic Party would uphold its belief in local self-government, and cease the Truman effort to socialize our economy and regiment our people.

"As the campaign progressed, I found I was wrong. The Democratic candidate lost no time in deserting the beliefs he said he had before his nomination...Before long he let Truman take over his campaign hook, line and sinker, and climbed in bed with a motley crew of Socialists, political parasites and South-haters."

To my knowledge, Daddy became the first, and the only Democratic Member of Congress to openly support Dwight D. Eisenhower in 1952.

He praised Eisenhower for the organization in Europe that the General had "brought into being for the defense of the Western world, his executive ability, his flair for diplomacy." In addition, Daddy felt that the U.S. involvement in the Korean War was a direct result of weak, temporizing foreign policy decisions—Democratic decisions—since the close of World War II. Always an ardent supporter of a strong military and a strong defense, he hoped that Eisenhower would improve our postures in foreign relations as well as in domestic programs.

He declared that his vote for Eisenhower was "a vote for the Republic, not for Republicans."

It took courage politically for Daddy to come out publicly and say what he did. He knew that his stand would not be viewed kindly by the Democratic leadership in Congress and that he could well lose his seat on the Armed Services Committee, a genuine concern. "If this means reprisals against me as a Democrat," he said, "I can take the consequences. As a Congressman, I am expendable, but the United States of America and its future is not expendable."

Daddy received strong statewide support for his stand for Eisenhower and for ignoring the dictates of his own party leaders, with whom he disagreed. It was not the way to play the political game, but Daddy lived up to his reputation for being independent. It was by an extremely small margin that Stevenson received South Carolina's electoral votes.

It seems to be one of the ironies of politics that Eisenhower had been approached by some Democrats to run for President on their party's ticket in 1948.

Political reality set in soon after the election, though, for Mendel Rivers the Democrat who had chosen to support a Republican. Daddy did not lose his seat on the Armed Services Committee, but he found out quickly that it was not like-minded philosophies that counted in the real world, but politics as usual.

Republican "thanks" came in the form of no thanks at all. Many of Daddy's patronage privileges were stripped from him. Political patronage appointments—postmasters, customs collectors, federal marshals and the like—traditionally are given to Members of Congress of the *same* party as the administration in power. Even though Daddy had stuck his political neck out for the Republican party, and Eisenhower in particular, his patronage privileges were assigned to someone else to dispense. The nephew of a Republican senator moved to Charleston and it was he who made the decisions about patronage appointments.

Daddy said he'd never go out on a limb for another Republican. And he never did.

Actually, Daddy probably was not surprised by the Republican action. The Executive Branch clearly sees the patronage issue as a privilege, not a right. The Democratic Administration of Truman had taken away many of his patronage privileges a few years earlier when he had failed to support Truman in 1948.

Nonetheless, Daddy took that rebuff in characteristic stride and got along well with Eisenhower on many issues when he was in office. Shortly after the inauguration in 1953, Daddy visited the new President in the White House to discuss matters regarding the war going on in Korea, taking some golf balls along as a gift for Eisenhower, an avid golfer. They may not have been political allies on all counts, but they shared the same views on anti-Communism and they both enjoyed golf. Years later when Daddy became Chairman of the Armed Services Committee, Eisenhower paid Daddy a visit—rendering receptionist Kathy Worthington speechless as he suddenly appeared unannounced—

bearing a gift of golf balls for the new Chairman.

Daddy had his share of disagreements with the Eisenhower Administration. Whether it was cuts in the defense budget or details of a piece of civil rights legislation, Daddy was often in the thick of the battle.

Civil rights legislation, of course, continued to fire up the country and the Congress throughout the 1950s and 1960s—Daddy included. In 1957, especially, Daddy became very vocal about including a right-to-work amendment in the civil rights legislation then under consideration. During hearings on the bill, Judiciary Committee Chairman Emmanuel Cellar of New York accused Daddy of seeking to destroy not only unions but the civil rights bill as well. But Daddy maintained that the right to have a job and earn a living "is just as basic a civil right as any that Mr. Cellar or anyone else can name..."

Defending the right-to-work laws in many states, including South Carolina, he said that they were proper "because it is not just the right of government, but its duty, to protect the basic right of any man to hold a job if he is qualified to hold it."

Daddy also spoke strongly against provisions of the bill which denied trial by jury for individuals suspected of attempting to deprive others of their civil rights. It was, in Daddy's opinion, "the most fantastic concoction that has ever been presented to a parliamentary legislative body. You abolish our judicial system as we have it...This is more power than a good government should want and a bad government should have."

Interestingly enough, Congressman Adam Clayton Powell, generally considered the Congressional spokesman for the NAACP (which largely supported the bill), was in agreement with many of the opponents of the proposed legislation, many of whom were Southern whites. Declaring it to be too vague, Powell agreed with Daddy and others that to permit court action against persons seemingly "about to engage" in actions was to deny to someone his civil rights and amounted to "thought control."

Not surprisingly, Daddy and Powell, who represented New York's Harlem area, were generally poles apart on just about everything.

However, their names were mentioned together from time to time during the Eisenhower years because both Democrats had failed to support their party's presidential ticket. Mendel Rivers was not "disciplined" for his support of Eisenhower in 1952 and the Democrats felt, consequently, that they could not very well censure Powell for his support of the Republican in 1956—an action many said Powell took to get Justice Department pressure off of members of his staff involved in tax irregularity indictments.

Daddy had decidedly not supported Eisenhower in the 1956 election: "You can bet I didn't vote for him in 1956. There ain't no education in the second kick of a mule!" he said later when asked about his vote.

For all the numerous controversies surrounding Adam Clayton Powell (and there were many), he, a rather privileged black, won many battles for blacks on his charm and wit alone. When he went to Congress in 1945, he blatantly broke many "Whites Only" rules in Washington, including the implied and accepted one for the dining room "Reserved for Members of Congress Only." As a fierce champion of the NAACP, Powell made a rather unexpected personal observation in his book *Adam by Adam*:

"I've always respected a white Southerner more than a white Northerner. A white Northerner is one who says openly that he has no prejudice and yet practices it every day of his life. The white Southerner is the one who says, 'I am prejudiced, but I have certain friends I would do anything in the world for.' In other words one is a hypocrite and the other is bluntly honest."

Daddy could get along well with just about everyone with whom he served in Congress, including the flamboyant and sometimes arrogant Powell, whom he frequently criticized publicly.

Mother told me that in 1970 she and Daddy ran into Powell in the tiny airport on the island of Bimini where he had gone to live after a tumultuous Congressional scandal over an alleged misuse of funds. Daddy and Powell greeted each other warmly. Having not met him before, Mother said that she was greatly impressed by his gentle, courteous manner and his personal charm.

CHAPTER 8

No one ever accused Mendel Rivers of being lazy!

He was totally absorbed by his job as Congressman. When he had pledged in 1940 "to work for my people," he had meant it with a vengeance.

The small *North Charleston Banner* gave this assessment of his career: "'Rivers Delivers' was a factual and, therefore powerful slogan...but another slogan...truly described the man...'Your Congressman.'"

If his predecessor in Congress had sometimes been accused of being inaccessible, no one could say that Daddy was unavailable to his constituents.

In 1941, he initiated regularly-scheduled district-wide trips during which he would meet with groups and individuals. One-on-one meetings with constituents is certainly routine procedure now for any politician who wants to be re-elected, but back then it was a new idea, at least in the First Congressional District of South Carolina.

It took months for his office staff to work out the details of the annual district trips, and his constituents counted on them. Hundreds of letters would go out to people all over the First District announcing the dates, and the response was always heavy. He would generally go to a county courthouse or county office building and personally visit with as many people as feasible.

"His annual district trip was pure Americana," a newspaper account later said. "A close associate described it as 'the savior coming home.'

Rivers would spend a day in each county seat and people would come in with personal problems involving the government.

"They ranged from red tape about Social Security to getting a boy in service closer to home because a parent was seriously ill. An aide dutifully took notes and the complaints were acted on back in Washington.

"'He liked to think of himself as a country boy,' an associate recalls, 'and the trips were a source of strength to him.'"

They were also very good politics.

As much as possible, he readily accepted invitations to speak to various groups throughout the district and state, business organizations, civic clubs, military groups, agricultural clubs, political gatherings and schools on all levels. His constituency was an important audience and he enjoyed making newsworthy "major" announcements when speaking in South Carolina, rather than from his office in Washington.

On many occasions, he would invite well-known personalities to come to functions in the district—astronauts, sports figures and many prominent military and political people. He never, to my knowledge, failed to attend the Hampton County Watermelon Festival, which drew crowds of 10,000 to this rural part of the district. It was there that he had made his first campaign speech in 1940. When the Festival was dedicated to him in 1965, its organizer, Corrin Bowers, even wrote a glowing poem in praise of his Congressman. Astronauts John Young, Gus Grissom and John Glenn accompanied Daddy to the festivities.

"Any politician has a lot of constituents," it was once told to me, "but Mendel's people weren't constituents. They were always friends. He knew the difference."

Most of Daddy's constituents called him "Mendel," not "Congressman Rivers," and he liked it that way. He had a truly phenomenal memory and could remember, seemingly without effort, the names, faces and personal details about almost everyone he ever met.

On one occasion, though, at a Citadel football game, a man came up to Daddy and, in a loud voice, showing off for his listening companions (who evidently had a bet riding on the response from the Congressman), demanded as he tugged on Daddy's sleeve, "Mendel, what's my name? What's my name?"

"Well, if you don't know your own name," Daddy replied, annoyed at being toyed with, "then how do you expect me to know it? You'd better get a dog tag to put around your neck."

Over the years he increased the number of permanent staff members in the Charleston office and encouraged constituents to call upon his staff for assistance. It was unusual in Charleston at the time for a federal representative to have more than a skeleton office staff except around election time. After Daddy became Chairman of the Armed Services Committee, and therefore more powerful, people from all over South Carolina and nearby states sought help through the district office.

His staff members were much more than remarkable. He expected and got a great deal from them. Coralee Bull, who worked for him for 14 years, said that when she interviewed for the job, she never thought it would work out. "He was *very* demanding, but somehow you delivered. But he was demanding for good reasons."

He did not like "stupid" mistakes (which he pronounced in an exaggerated, long, drawn-out "stuuuuupid") and could let one know of his displeasure with a stern look and his left eyebrow raised. Two secretaries routinely took dictation from him at the same time to be fairly assured that no errors were made. His staff was generally able, fortunately, to keep a sense of humor and take things pretty much in stride. They seemed to be utterly loyal and fond of him.

The volume of mail coming into his office kept increasing over the years and the staff worked under the strict instruction to answer every letter the day it arrived in the office. At one point, after he became Chairman, it was reported that his office received more mail than any other Congressional office.

Mendel Davis, who worked for Daddy for several years, told me that occasionally the staff would neglect to untie a bundle of mail because doing so would have kept them in the office half the night answering it. Instead, they simply dropped the unopened bundle back down the mail chute, unbeknownst to their boss, so that it would have to be re-delivered the next day.

I often wonder what Daddy's reaction would have been if he had known that a new, inexperienced secretary answered the telephone one day and was overheard to say: "Congressman Rivers' office...The president of what, please?...Oh, the President of the United States...(long pause)...Hot Dawg!"

My father had boundless energy and it started up early in the morning. Some accused him of having insomnia and being unable to sleep, but, whatever the reason, he insisted that he liked to get up early "to get a jump on the day before it gets a jump on you." I never knew him to sleep past 5 a.m., but Mother said that he frequently was up at 3:30 or 4:00. He was usually quiet during those early hours and would be careful not to awaken his sleeping family.

Mother and many other people, however, didn't always share Daddy's fondness for the wee hours of the morning. He loved to place telephone calls to close friends and associates early, and somehow he could usually get away with the practice. (About the only person who ever admitted to enjoying the pre-dawn conversations was Frank Boykin, Daddy's colleague from Alabama).

Mother said that one of the best things she ever did for her marriage was to put an extension telephone in the basement of one of the houses they lived in.

Joe Riley said that Daddy routinely called from Washington by 6 a.m. to ask "Have you read the paper yet?," eager to learn the type of coverage that had been given to something or other. When Joe, suddenly awakened, protested, Daddy would say: "Well, you're awake now, so go on down and read me what the paper has to say."

Joe told me (in good humor, I hope) that Daddy nearly ruined his health *and* his marriage with his early morning phone calls. His wife, Helen, told him that she "didn't care if Mendel Rivers was running the country or not, he'd better stop calling so early in the morning."

Newspaper carrier Leon Cooper said in an interview that he had tried to accommodate all of his customers but was unable to please Daddy's friend, Charleston Postmaster Roland Wooten during the 1960s:

"Mr. Wooten wanted me to bring him the first newspaper off the press. He said he had to have it that way so that he could read the news and compile a report for Rep. L. Mendel Rivers when he called by telephone at 5 a.m. from Washington. I told him I could not break my route to give him his service without inconveniencing other subscribers. He appealed to Mr. Williams [the circulation manager], who supported my decision. The postmaster stopped speaking to both of us."

Daddy once called an electrician at 6 a.m. to ask why he hadn't arrived yet to do some repair job. Surprisingly, the electrician has only fond memories of my father.

There may have been some people in the district whom Daddy called early who, while surprised at the hour, were flattered to receive a call from their Congressman who sought their opinion on some matter. Most others were probably furious.

Daddy would frequently schedule meetings and interviews for an hour when most people would normally just be having their first cup of coffee. Many newspaper and magazine writers learned that the only time they could interview him was very early, usually 7 a.m.

One of the things that my father was eager to experience first-hand was piloting an airplane. He was, however, 60 years old when he finally got around to trying it. Several of his friends were accomplished pilots, and, having learned a great deal about various airplanes over the years, he was convinced that he, too, could master the basics of the skill.

He brought up the subject with Frank Jameson, in whose small twin-engined plane he sometimes travelled. Frank and Daddy, despite a 20-year gap in their ages, had developed a close personal relationship over several years. A dedicated former Navy pilot and prominent figure in the aerospace industry, Frank held many of the same views as did Daddy on issues affecting national defense. Like many of Daddy's close friends, Frank was a Republican. They were good enough friends to be able to enjoy their disagreements just as easily as their agreements. Frank became one of Daddy's most ardent admirers. The feeling was mutual.

One of their disagreements was about flying. Frank's first thought when Daddy told him that he wanted to learn to fly was: "Mother of God...I tried to dissuade him and told him he shouldn't do it but he was determined. He had his mind made up and wouldn't listen to any of my arguments. He had no idea about the time and money involved in learning to fly." But, since Frank was his friend, he determined that the best thing he could do was to help him by making certain that he got the proper airplane and the proper training.

Reluctantly, Frank agreed to sell his personal plane, a Beechcraft Bonanza, which he had maintained with loving care for years, to Daddy for a bargain price. He even had his personal pilot, Ray Cote, come to Washington for several weeks to spend as much time as possible with Daddy while he learned the basics. Every morning, very early, Daddy and Ray would get out in the plane for their sessions together. Daddy was given special permission, Frank told me, to use one of the runways at National Airport in Washington during the very early morning hours to practice take-offs and landings.

Former South Carolina Congressman, then U.S. District Judge, Bob Hemphill, also spurred Daddy on. He had taken up flying some years before and was enthusiastic when he learned Daddy was interested. He recommended his own former flying teacher in the Washington area who could be available, fitting Daddy's schedule, for lessons.

Daddy was also receiving encouragement from Roland Wooten, the Postmaster in Charleston, an Ace pilot in World War II, who frequently took Daddy on short trips in his own small plane. Roland, a graduate of The Citadel, had flown hundreds of combat missions during the war before being shot down and wounded. Returning to the United States as a highly-decorated hero, he spent his recuperation time selling War Bonds all over the country with former heavyweight champion Jack Dempsey, with whom he became a fast friend. Later, he volunteered to return to Europe, and flew a short time before being shot down again and imprisoned for the duration of the war. He became the most decorated alumnus of The Citadel in World War II.

At one point, Daddy and Roland talked about the possibility of owning a plane jointly but could not agree about whether to keep the plane in Charleston or in Washington for the majority of the time.

Mother was completely against the idea.

To her great relief, Daddy ultimately decided against becoming a pilot and keeping the airplane. Frank told me that a frightening experience during a thunderstorm was a contributing factor in giving Daddy second thoughts about flying. In addition, he realized that his increasingly busy schedule could not accommodate such an indulgence. Roland bought the Bonanza and kept it in Charleston.

In 1968, Daddy and Roland flew together to attend the Daytona 500 stock car races in that same airplane. Daddy was a frequent visitor to the Daytona Speedway at the invitation of Bill France, the NASCAR president. He had been the guest speaker for festivities there honoring winners of the Congressional Medal of Honor and had on a few occasions ridden in the lead pace car at the beginning of the races. (He was a fast driver himself.) Daddy was named NASCAR Commissioner the year before he died.

Rather than fly back to Charleston with Roland, Daddy returned to Washington with Transportation Secretary Alan Boyd. A few hours after his arrival there, he learned that Roland had died when his plane had gone down on its approach into Charleston.

In the great confusion that often surrounds such tragedies, members of Daddy's staff were unable to determine for several hours whether he had been on the plane with Roland or not. They were finally convinced when an official at the private airline terminal in Washington told them that he thought Mr. Rivers had arrived because there had been "a man with long white hair fussing about how his luggage had been handled" earlier in the evening.

Living and working with a man like Mendel Rivers was sometimes difficult to the point of frustration. We always knew that he would generally get more upset over the small things than the big things. Mother came to accept the fact that, with the pressures of his work, he needed to be able to blow off steam from time to time. But, once vented, his outbursts were quickly concluded.

He was generous, sometimes to a fault. He never failed to bring home gifts from his frequent travels for his family (and often for many friends and staff members, as well)...even if only something very small. One time, though, after several attempts to please Mother with a coat, she accepted one with high praise, in appreciation for his efforts. He promptly order another *exactly* like it for her since she seemed to like it so much.

Some gifts were even harder to deal with—like the dog! For some time Daddy had expressed an interest in having a dog, not having had a pet for a number of years. Mother agreed that a small one might be acceptable with their more demanding schedules, for companionship as well as for protection. But before Mother could protest, Daddy accepted a German Shepherd puppy from a friend and presented it to her.

The dog arrived in Charleston and Daddy left Mother and the puppy together almost immediately and returned to business in Washington. For several weeks, during an unusually bitter cold snap, Mother tried to housebreak the young dog, attempting to interest him in the cold outdoors rather than in the warmth of the inside of the house—and her rugs. She said that her efforts were largely unsuccessful and, in desperation, she finally telephoned Daddy in Washington:

"Mendel, this dog is making my life miserable. I'm getting nowhere with him. You'll have to make a decision," she announced, firmly. "It's either me or the dog!"

"Well, darling, I'm sorry that you haven't learned to love the little thing. I was certain that you would be friends by now," he said. "I'll take the dog."

After several terms in Congress, Daddy began hosting what became his annual "Bird Luncheon." At first, they were rather small affairs, held in one of the dining rooms in the Capitol. Over the years the luncheons grew and grew until several hundred people were often in attendance, including Members of Congress, high-ranking military brass, cabinet members, industrialists, sports figures and dozens of friends and supporters from South Carolina. He put together a menu which showed off some of the finest cuisine from Daddy's district, including Charleston's "She-Crab Soup" and quail from the South Carolina Lowcountry. It was an opportunity for his friends from home to mix with his friends from Washington. No one enjoyed it more than Daddy did.

Loyal friends and relatives in the district were called upon to help. Sometimes it wasn't easy.

Daddy once called his brother-in-law, Harold Odom (Blanche's husband), and announced: "I'm having a luncheon for some important people the day after tomorrow. You'll have plenty of time to go fishing tomorrow and I'll need at least twenty pounds of good fish."

"Mendel," Harold protested, "I can't guarantee you that I can catch 20 pounds of fish tomorrow."

"Oh, sure you can! Just see that they are on the plane by two o'clock so that I can get the chef to prepare them. Thanks."

Although planning to play golf rather than fish, Harold went fishing the next day. He caught a few fish but knew that he could never meet the deadline. He didn't want to disappoint his demanding brother-in-law, of whom he was quite fond. So he went to a local fish market and purchased several pounds of fish to make up the difference, packed them in dry ice and delivered them to the air freight terminal with little time to spare.

Daddy called him later that day full of praise and appreciation: "You didn't think you could do it, eh? I'll tell my guests what great brothers-in-law we have in Charleston!"

Harold never told Daddy the truth.

Daddy often prevailed upon his sister Blanche, who operated a large florist business in Charleston, to organize the collection of camellias from gardens to be shipped up to Washington for the Bird Luncheon or some other special occasion. Once he called her when Charleston was enduring one of its rare cold spells and told her that he needed a quantity of the blooms—within two days time.

"Mendel, you're crazy! There's snow on the ground here. All my camellias are brown."

"Well, I know you can find some somewhere. Ask your friends," he prevailed.

She did, and, amazingly, they were able to find some blooms that had been protected from the cold. They were carefully packed in large boxes and shipped to Washington.

Daddy loved to give camellias to colleagues from colder climates, gently reminding them that his part of the country was always lovely, even in the dead of winter.

For a time, the Bird Luncheons were held in honor of all the members of the Joint Chiefs of Staff. But after becoming Chairman, Daddy honored one individual at the luncheon—one time General Mark Clark and another time Jack Dempsey. Several times, then House Speaker John McCormack was the guest of honor. Daddy and Mr. McCormack were special friends and often joked that they were the only two members of the McCormack-crat Party and would not allow anyone else to join.

Once, when I was staying with him just after he became Chairman, he asked me to attend as his hostess in Mother's absence. He was at his best. I was very impressed as he, with no prompting whatsoever, introduced each individual of the over two hundred present, never faltering for a name and a distinguishing anecdote about the person.

Daddy generally had his staff set up a bar in his office for his Bird Luncheon guests so that they could enjoy a drink beforehand, if desired. Coralee Bull told me that occasionally a small group would stop by for a few minutes. Daddy, she said, was never in his office before the luncheons and it was up to her and other staff members to act as hosts for him. On one occasion, Billy Graham stopped by, but not for a drink. He asked Mrs. Bull if he might use Daddy's private bathroom to change clothes before the luncheon, as he had just finished playing golf with the President. Mrs. Bull stalled him in the outer reception offfice just long enough for another staff member to get into Daddy's office through an inner door and get all of the liquor out of sight. Then, she ushered him into Daddy's office.

Daddy wanted everybody who visited his office to sign his guestbook, and it was the responsibility of his staff to see that it was done. Several days after Billy Graham had come and gone from the luncheon, Daddy questioned Mrs. Bull as to why Dr. Graham's signature was not in his guestbook for that day. He could not understand why anyone in his office could have failed in this small task. "Because, Mr. Rivers," she told him, "I was too busy hiding liquor in your office to have him sign the guest book."

At the last luncheon that he hosted in 1970, my brother Mendel, then a student at Georgetown University, was invited. Mendel, sporting muttonchop whiskers, drove his 1947 Dodge (which he had restored to perfection) into the Rayburn House Office Building circular driveway and confidently parked it among the limousines of the VIPs. He was quickly challenged by a Capitol policeman. Once he had established his identity, he was allowed to leave his car there.

Daddy genuinely enjoyed being with "his people" whether in the district or in Washington. He took pleasure in taking constituents to lunch in the House Dining Room and making the necessary arrangements for a visit to watch the proceedings on the floor from the House Gallery when Congress was in session.

It was no chore for him to meet early arriving trains at Union Station when friends came to Washington. G.G. Dowling from Beaufort, who would serve as his last district-wide campaign manager in 1970, recalled that "Mendel, as was well known, practically lived in his office the whole time he was in Washington...On many occasions when I arrived in Washington at 6:40 a.m. on the overnight train he was there to meet me and often we had breakfast in his office with Mendel scrambling the eggs on his own electric unit."

Daddy frequently went beyond the expected. When Charles "Pug" Ravenel, a Charlestonian, was a White House Fellow, he asked Daddy if he could sit in on an Armed Services Committee hearing. Daddy was proud of the young man who had earned a newspaper scholarship to attend prep school and had gone on to distinguish himself as a Harvard student and quarterback. Since Pug had Top Secret Clearance, Daddy invited him to be present at a closed session where Defense Secretary McNamara and the Joint Chiefs of Staff would be testifying.

McNamara was to be the first witness to speak. Daddy said "Good Morning" to the Secretary who responded in kind and proceeded to begin to read his testimony.

Almost immediately, Daddy interrupted him and said: "Excuse me, Mr. Secretary, but I want to take this opportunity to introduce you, the Joint Chiefs and the members of my committee to one of my esteemed constituents, Mr. Pug Ravenel." The Secretary and the Joint Chiefs were surprised by the interruption and Pug remembered that he was embarrassed, but pleasantly embarrassed. After Pug's introduction, Daddy said to McNamara: "Now, Mr. Secretary, you may begin."

After returning to live in Charleston, Pug was a Democratic candidate for Congress for the First Congressional District many years later.

Daddy could, and did, take a large measure of the credit for vastly improving the economic conditions of his district and the state throughout the years he served in Congress.

There was, admittedly, much room for growth and development in South Carolina and the South as a whole when Daddy was first elected. Whenever possible, he encouraged, nurtured and worked to see that his district, his state and his region of the country tap their unrealized potentials. Part of his success stems from the fact that his district has some obviously favorable conditions with which to work, including a coastal location, a mild year-round climate, a willing labor market and a tradition of local business and government cooperation.

A former head of the Charleston Development Board, William Humphreys, told me that from the beginning of Daddy's career in Washington, he was a valuable asset to Charleston industry. "He was approachable, responsive and most helpful, and as time went by and his importance grew, so grew his Washington reach...Few manufacturers and none of us developers would think of approaching any federal agency without Mendel's involvement...

"Mendel wasn't bashful in pushing Charleston as a prime location for industry, and his friends in industry listened because they would have liked to put investments in his district. Trouble was, cold-blooded engineering and economic analyses usually showed there were good reasons we were not as good or fit as some place else. The important thing was, Mendel opened doors for us and companies looked at Charleston seriously which otherwise wouldn't have come near us. He gave us the opportunity of presenting Charleston, which was all we were entitled to, and we at least had the satisfaction of knowing we weren't passed over because of something the company misunderstood or was not aware of.

"Some of Mendel's most valuable work for the manufacturing industry was with support activities such as construction of the Bushy Park project [an industrial park complex] and development of the port."

Daddy is best remembered for his accomplishments in connection with many defense-related installations. There was indeed a dramatic build-up in military facilities in the First Congressional District of South Carolina during Mendel Rivers' career in Congress. For the most part, he was tremendously successful in his efforts to enlarge existing military facilities and add several others, efforts which changed the economic picture markedly in the Charleston area.

It was said by some of his friends and associates that Daddy was often embarrassed and sometimes genuinely amused by all the credit given to him for the military build-up in his district during his years in Congress. More often, he took the recognition in stride. Once, at ceremonies marking the expansion of a defense-oriented plant in Charleston, Daddy told the audience: "I have to admit that I had nothing to do with bringing the...plant to Charleston," a remark which drew a stunned silence from those present. Then he added, "Of course, I don't admit anything like that during an election year."

The economy in the First Congressional District was so vastly changed during his years in Congress that some people referred to the rivers in Charleston as "the Ashley, the Cooper and the Mendel...all of which come together to form the Atlantic Ocean."

The military itself, especially the Navy, was anxious to move or establish facilities in the South and take advantage of the cheaper land and labor, not to mention the weather.

The Navy Yard in Charleston was established in 1901, four years before Daddy's birth, and he had lived very near it as a boy growing up in North Charleston.

"Because the Navy Yard at Charleston is the only sizable Navy Yard south of Hampton Roads," he said in his first congressional campaign in 1940, "there is every reason to feel that facilities should be furnished the Charleston Navy Yard so that every type of vessel up to and including the battleship type could be dry-docked for repairs...I am sure that the merchants and business men in this district will cooperate with me in further expanding this vital implement of defense, which is already Charleston's principal industry, with a weekly payroll of approximately $150,000."

When, in 1949, as part of the Administration's economy drive, the shipyard was threatened with closure, it took tremendous effort on the part of Daddy, South Carolina's Senators, the Charleston business community (led by Joe Riley) and many others to save it. Daddy always had great faith that the naval facility could and would be a great one, not only because it was in his district, but also because of its strategic value to the U.S. defense system. He never let up in his efforts to broaden the scope of its activities which ultimately included major drydock installations and the location in Charleston of a multi-million dollar Polaris missile assembly and submarine facility. He would have been heartbroken had he lived to see the government decide, in 1993, to close the Charleston naval base and naval shipyard.

Charleston Harbor, plagued by a silting problem, has to be constantly maintained, an effort which was and is vital to accommodate the movement of ships and submarines to and from the Naval Base. Daddy worked with federal agencies to keep the harbor properly dredged and to begin the construction of a re-diversion canal at the major source of the problem, efforts which affected the active civilian shipping industry, and South Carolina's overall economy, as well. At one time he urged the building of a tunnel beneath the Cooper River, the major shipping channel and the route to the naval facilities. The uninterrupted strategic activities of the shipyard needed protection, he argued, in case of an enemy attack on the bridge crossing this vital river.

Workers at the shipyard knew that they could count on their Congressman to help them if need be. James Grayson, of the shipyard's Metal Trades Council, told a newspaper interviewer about a time that Daddy's assistance was sought when the yard was slated for a "RIF" (reduction in force) in 1964: "A group of us went to Washington, saw Rivers and discussed the situation. Rivers called Vinson [Carl Vinson, then Chairman of the Armed Services Committee] and said, 'Carl, I want to see President Johnson—now.'

"Then he told us to come back at 2 p.m. When we went back he told us to go on back to Charleston, that a ship would be pulling in for enough work to reduce the "RIF." And he told us we had better hurry or the ship would beat us there.

As the Navy became more nuclear oriented, so did the support systems at the Charleston facility. Once, when proficiency ratings were low at the Shipyard, Daddy asked Admiral Hyman G. Rickover, the so-called Father of the Nuclear Navy, to come to Charleston. The feisty Admiral, respected for his no-nonsense approach to things *and* for his brilliance, gave the workers a "pep talk," which I am certain must have made a strong impression. Ratings, I was told, went up considerably after that.

By the end of the 1960s, the Charleston Naval Shipyard had become one of the most important naval facilities in the country.

Another major military facility, the Charleston Air Force Base, was a small troop carrier installation until it was made a temporary part of the Military Air Transport Service (MATS) in 1953.

Understandably, Daddy pushed for the base to be designated a permanent rather than a temporary one—a change which would virtually guarantee growth and longevity. "Take it from me," he boasted at the time, "big things are in store for the Charleston Air Force Base." He was right.

It took, however, nearly two years for the City of Charleston, which owned the land and shared the runways with the air base, to come to an agreement with the Air Force regarding the terms of the final sale (unencumbered ownership being a federal requirement for a facility to be made "permanent"). Daddy was, naturally, caught in the middle of what were sometimes heated discussions as the City sought to protect its own long-term prospects. In the end, both parties were satisfied with the final results which Daddy termed "the most liberal joint usage agreement that the Air Force has in the nation."

Several years later Daddy was appointed to serve as the chairman of a subcommittee to investigate the "capabilities and needs" of MATS. Many attempts were being made in the late 1950s to make vast changes in the structure of all military branches, including the function of MATS. For one, private airlines endeavored to take over the bulk of military cargo and passenger transportation and lobbied strenuously on Capitol Hill to allow them to do so. Daddy was firmly opposed.

In committee hearings, an Air Transport Association witness (speaking for the private airlines) contended that MATS was merely "a government airline." On the contrary, Daddy argued, MATS was "a combat force, in training in peacetime to do a job in wartime." He accused the private airlines of wanting to haul "selective cargo and personnel...the easy, high payload job. They're willing to leave the hard and dangerous jobs to MATS, but we are not. Their program could have no other result than to render impotent, as a military force, MATS as we know it, and I can assure you that the subcommittee will not stand for this."

MATS remained part of the military.

One of the commanders of the Air Force Base during its early years, General Franklin Henley, said that Daddy frequently flew to Europe on transport planes out of Charleston wanting to study the situation of MATS from the men who were actually involved. "This was not luxurious travel. What he saw first hand," said General Henley, "was that some of the planes used in the late 1950s—C-121s and 124s—were perfectly suited for peacetime civilian passenger and routine cargo transport, but unadaptable to wartime military needs." Daddy pushed for the mammoth C141s, C-4s and the C-5s. By the time of the Vietnam crisis, MATS had been put to the test in many parts of the world and handled the requirements of massive movements of troops and materiel with virtual ease.

In June of 1970, the first of the goliath C-5 Galaxy transport planes made its public debut at the Charleston Air Force Base. Massive cost overruns during its development and production had made it one of the most controversial aircrafts ever to make it into the air. My father had long pushed for an airplane with its capabilities; the U.S. Air Force would now have the unassailable ability to airlift tanks, fighter aircraft and helicopters to distances of 3000 miles at the speed of over 450 knots per hour. He considered the plane's production to be essential to our military strength and he had never wavered in his support. Some people joked that Mendel Rivers acted personally responsible for the plane and dubbed it the "C-5 Mendel."

Daddy was, of course, the main speaker for the reception ceremonies that day at the Air Base. The ceremony was held on the ramp near a recently-completed hangar, designed specifically to house the huge craft. Hundreds of people were on hand to witness the event.

In perfect sync with my father's remarks to the crowd, the C-5 approached the runway. All eyes were on that already-famous plane.

As it touched down, one of the main wheels broke loose and, at 120 miles per hour, chased the giant aircraft down the runway!

When the noise of the aircraft and the stunned crowd died down, Daddy, absolutely unruffled, turned to the hundreds assembled and announced: "That's the reason we put 28 wheels on that plane. We can lose a few and never miss 'em."

The training school for the C-5 was originally planned to be at the Charleston Air Force Base, as well. That is, until my father learned that the Altus Air Force Base in Oklahoma was to be closed, thereby shutting down the military community as well as the surrounding civilian community. He quietly had the legislative authorization bill changed to designate Altus rather than his hometown of Charleston (which translated into jobs and money) for the school to train the plane's crews. So grateful were the recipients of that gesture that a "Mendel Rivers Week" (not merely "Day") was held in his honor; even the elementary school was named for him.

In the first Defense Authorization Bill that Daddy authored after becoming Chairman, he wrote the provision to change MATS to MAC—Military Airlift Command. Not only did military airlift gain a position of greater importance in the defense structure by becoming a command, but it also "greatly improved the morale of the personnel," said General Henley—always an important consideration for Daddy.

One evening Daddy received a telephone call at home from an extremely irate constituent. The caller was quite annoyed about the noise of the airplanes flying in and out of the Charleston Air Force Base. For several minutes, Daddy patiently listened to the woman's tirade, then he calmly asked her:

"Are they American planes?"

"Yes, sir, of course, they are," she answered.

"Well, then, you better thank God that they are, and not Russian ones!" he shot back.

Carl Vinson once cautioned Daddy: "Mendel, if you put any more military installations in your district, it's going to sink."

Daddy was sometimes even credited with the establishment of the Marine Corps recruit training depot at Parris Island, near Beaufort, but it had been established some 14 years before his birth. He did, however, have a significant hand in writing legislation for the Beaufort Naval

Hospital and the Naval Air Station there.

Daddy enjoyed telling the tongue-in-cheek story about how he got the Veterans Administration Hospital to be built in Charleston, although it had been slated originally to be built in Columbia. He said that it paid off to be on speaking terms with the President. According to Daddy, he met with then President John F. Kennedy and had this conversation:

"Why can't you build the hospital at Charleston, Mr. President?"

"You've got nothing to build it on but a mud flat," answered Kennedy.

"All of Charleston is built on a mud flat. The buildings rest on pilings and the sewer lines do, too. We can secure the land," Daddy argued.

Finally, Kennedy called in an aide and ordered the release of $200,000 in funds to prepare plans to build the hospital in Charleston.

"And that's what I mean about being on speaking terms with the President."

Daddy then persuaded the President to have a submarine named for South Carolina statesman John C. Calhoun. He was about to ask Kennedy for one last thing when the President stopped him: "Don't press your luck too far, Mendel!"

While he didn't agree with Kennedy on many issues, he enjoyed a cordial relationship with him and enjoyed telling stories about the conversations between the two of them.

Arthur Ravenel said that Daddy related having once asked Kennedy how he enjoyed being President. "Well, it's great," replied the President, "except for one thing. It makes it very hard to do any slipping around."

"Well, what you need to do, Mr. President," Daddy offered, "is to change all those Secret Service *men* to Secret Service *women*."

"That's the best suggestion I've had since I've been President." Kennedy reportedly replied.

When, at the height of anti-military protests in the 1960s, Daddy was accused of having made his home district a "microcosm of the military-industrial complex," he said: "Charleston happens to be a great, natural warm water port. It was made that way by God—whom, I presume, is not a captive of the military-industrial complex."

When the District of Columbia Chapter of the Air Force

Association honored Daddy with a luncheon, Vice President Spiro Agnew told the crowd of 3,000 who had come to pay him this high tribute:

"I would like to lay to rest the ugly, vicious, dastardly rumor that he is trying to move the Pentagon piecemeal to South Carolina...I have had it clearly explained to me that the military facilities so evident in that area are a testament of Mendel Rivers' unselfish willingness to allow his own district of South Carolina to accept, in the national interest, military installations which just had to be put someplace...Even when it looked like Charleston might sink into the sea from the burden, Mendel Rivers' patriotic response was 'I regret that I have but one congressional district to give my country to—I mean, give to my country.'"

After being in Congress for a quarter of a century, Daddy pointed out that the large military and military-related payroll of hundreds of millions of dollars "would be the mainspring and heartbeat of the Charleston area as long as you can project the future. Without bragging, I can say that I have sponsored ninety percent of the military installations in the state." Known for his almost undivided attention to military affairs, he was frequently charged with being insensitive to "social programs." He responded by saying that giving people the means to have good jobs while working for the security of their country (which protected *all* jobs) was *his* kind of social agenda and he made no apologies for it.

When Daddy died in 1970, the annual military payroll in the Charleston area was $208 million.

Republican Arthur Ravenel once advised his party not to oppose Mendel Rivers for re-election, calling him "our greatest natural resource." Arthur, a cousin of my husband, was elected 16 years after Daddy's death to serve in the same seat in Congress.

A local columnist once noted that "our man, Mendel Rivers, hasn't been hurt by remaining loyal to the Democratic Party, despite the obvious surge of Conservatism, Republicanism and Goldwaterism in the Lowcountry...You couldn't beat Mendel at the polls with a 10-foot pole...This is borne out by the turnout in such First Congressional District Counties as Beaufort, Jasper and Hampton, where folks gathered in record numbers to pop questions at the white-maned chairman of the House Armed Services Committee...The Republicans would [not] think of running a candidate against Rivers in this congressional district...[it would be] a losing proposition."

On the national level, Daddy was frequently praised less by Democrats than by Republicans who agreed with his strong stands on national defense and his conservatism. Many people have told me that he was urged to change to the Republican Party, and that one person who particularly encouraged him to do so was then-Congressman Gerald Ford. I do not know if there were ever any such serious conversations or contemplations, but Mr. Ford did recall in a letter to me, many years after Daddy's death, that they had a "long and close friendship...We worked together frequently, especially on legislation involving the Armed Forces. Both of us were 'hawks' and believed in a strong national defense program...Our views on domestic legislation were also quite similar, with an emphasis on a conservative fiscal policy."

Mother remembers that after Ford's election to Congress, Daddy frequently spoke highly of the new young Representative from Michigan, who had just moved into a home near my parents' home in Alexandria.

Daddy knew that a Democrat would not represent the conservative-minded and Republican-leaning First District forever. He once told Arthur Ravenel: "After I'm gone, the next Congressman from this district will be a Republican." He did not, of course, anticipate his sudden death while still in office and the strong sentiment held for him which contributed to the election of his namesake and Godson, a Democrat, to succeed him for ten years. Republicans have, however, been elected since that time.

The Republican administration of Richard Nixon often expressed approval of the views of the Democratic Chairman of the House Armed Services Committee—and showed its friendship.

When South Carolina's eminent statesman, James F. Byrnes, was approaching his 90th birthday (also his 63rd wedding anniversary) in the spring of 1969, President Nixon invited him to celebrate the important day at the White House. Governor Byrnes was forced to decline the invitation because of ill health, so the President decided that he would go to *his* home in Columbia to celebrate the occasion.

Jimmy Byrnes had had a brilliant career in government and was held in very high esteem. It was said that Byrnes, not Truman, had been Roosevelt's first choice as a running mate in 1944. He had distinguished himself as a Congressman, Senator and Supreme Court Justice before stepping down from the High Court in 1942, at Roosevelt's personal request, to become Director of Economic Stabilization (later the War Mobilization office). He accompanied Roosevelt to the Conference at Yalta in 1945, then served as Truman's Secretary of State until 1947 when, reportedly at odds with the President, he resigned and returned to South Carolina.

Daddy and several other political dignitaries—both Republican and Democrat—were invited, along with their wives, to accompany the President to visit the Byrneses, and then to continue on to the Kentucky Derby in Louisville the same afternoon.

On board the President's plane were South Carolina's Senators Thurmond and Hollings, Senator Everett Dirksen, Senator Mike Mansfield, Congressman Albert Watson (who represented Columbia) and several Members of Congress from Kentucky.

Daddy had recommended the purchase of Air Force One for use by the President when John F. Kennedy had been in office. It was his first trip aboard the plane, though, and, when asked by a reporter why he had not travelled on it before, he answered, "I've never been invited before."

During the flight from Washington to Columbia, the South Carolinians were seated with the Nixons in the prestigious forward cabin. Mother recalled that the President was an affable host and that he and the men enjoyed a lively conversation. She chatted with Mrs. Nixon for a while and remembered being impressed by the First Lady's honesty when she asked her something about White House protocol. Mrs. Nixon responded: "I really don't know. We haven't lived there long enough for me to know."

Huge crowds welcomed the President they had helped to elect the previous year. Governor McNair and Columbia Mayor Lester Bates provided an official reception upon arrival and thousands waved and cheered all along the route from the airport to the Byrnes' home.

After flying on to attend the races in Kentucky, the group arrived back in Washington late in the afternoon.

Daddy and Mother realized that they had time to round out the day by attending a party at the house my brother shared with several of his classmates. It was a "hippie" costume party, so they decided to dress the roles and tried to look like aging hippies. Mother recalled that on that Saturday evening, the crowds and traffic in the Georgetown section of Washington were particularly heavy as they inched their way along the streets. What, she thought several times, would the police think if there were a traffic mishap and they had to identify themselves? My brother and his friends announced that they were the most authentic-looking couple present at the party!

In addition to enthusiastically re-electing Daddy 16 times to go to bat for them in Washington, "his people" made many gestures of appreciation for what he had accomplished. He received numerous awards and citations from business, civic and military organizations around the country as well, not to mention several foreign governments. Mother's cypress-panelled library walls are covered with plaques and photographs from occasions on which Daddy was honored. What she cannot display, she has given to several libraries, friends and family.

It has always been a special source of pride to our family that a long stretch of highway was named for Daddy in 1948. Rivers Avenue is now a main thoroughfare going through the City of North Charleston.

Daddy always had a keen interest in good automobiles and good roads and had been instrumental in helping to get many thoroughfares paved in South Carolina in the early years that he was in Congress. Rivers Avenue was not only newly-paved, but it was also one of the first dual-lane highways in the state.

He was especially pleased that the highway bearing his name was near the area where he grew up. A street-lighting ceremony for Rivers Avenue was held in April of 1949. Daddy, wearing an enormous insulated glove, pulled the main switch for the 118 "white way" lights along the street. In those days, it had very little traffic and only a few small businesses established along it.

Rivers Avenue has become one of the most frequently-travelled streets in the area as the City of North Charleston has experienced rapid growth. Many of the military installations for which Daddy worked so strenuously throughout his career were built or expanded close to Rivers Avenue. One intersection, however, has had the rather dubious distinction of having the highest traffic accident rate in the state.

If someone referred to "the dual lane" or "Highway 52," rather than "Rivers Avenue," my father was quick to make the correction: "Call it by its right name."

In 1958, a district-wide committee was organized to hold a "Mendel Rivers Appreciation Day" in Charleston. On a Friday afternoon in May, Daddy and many honored guests arrived at the Charleston Air Force Base and were escorted to The Citadel to view a special dress parade by the cadets in his honor. Later, the Chamber of Commerce hosted an Armed Forces Day reception which was followed by a dinner at the Air Base.

On Saturday, a 35 car parade proceeded down King Street, Charleston's main shopping route, as Daddy, his family, local supporters and close Congressional and military friends rode by. High school and college bands from around the district played and marched. Nearly a hundred merchants had contributed $10,000 worth of gift certificates which were dropped in ping-pong balls from a helicopter flying over the parade route. After the parade, some 2,000 people attended a barbecue in Daddy's honor at the local football stadium, where Daddy could only offer a brief statement of thanks: "I am overwhelmed. What have I done to merit this?...All I have done is to represent you." What else could he say?

By this time, there was little question about what Mendel Rivers could and would do for "his people" or about his efforts on the national level.

When, later that year, Daddy had opposition in the general election, what his opponent said may have surprised many of the voters in the First District. In an apparent reference to Daddy's record of performance over the previous 18 years, he said: "...The working man and the veterans of our state are in urgent need of a friend and a fellow worker in the Congress...We need a loyal Christian...We need a larger National Guard and larger and better armed forces for our own defense and protection."

Accountant Fritz H. Kuck, rather sadly, received but one vote in that election.

Daddy's hometown of St. Stephen gave him a "Homecoming" a few years later in 1964. The day-long celebration was an especially touching experience. Our family was flown by helicopter the forty miles from Charleston to St. Stephen, where, when we landed, Daddy was greeted by a group of local kindergarten children holding placards welcoming him. The entire small town seemed to be on hand for the festivities. Hundreds of farmers, textile workers, housewives and children mingled with the local, state and national leaders who came to pay a tribute to the small town boy who had succeeded.

My father had never forgotten about the area where he had grown up. He visited the town frequently and enjoyed getting together with friends from his childhood who still lived there. He was instrumental in helping to bring some industry into the region. In 1956, he returned to the town to be the commencement speaker at St. Stephen High School whose graduating class numbered 11 students.

My sister and I unveiled a marker designating Mendel Rivers Road, which ran the two miles from the historic St. Stephen's Episcopal Church which Daddy had attended as a child to his former home that his father had built nearly 50 years before. Speaker after speaker praised him. We were treated to a catfish stew for lunch and a barbecue supper before departure. A group of high school students sang "Carolina in the Morning" when we visited Daddy's old home, then unoccupied, and wandered nostalgically from room to room.

One observer said of the occasion:

"Thousands of words of praise were heaped upon the silver-maned Congressman soon to become Chairman of the powerful House Armed Services Committee, but the biggest salute of all came from St. Stephen Mayor J. Smythe Rich who referred to him as 'still a country boy from Gumville.'

"That's what Gumvillians like most about Rep. Rivers. His great success as a politician and more important as a human being has left him basically the same as he was some 50 years ago when he tramped through Hell Hole Swamp in his bare feet."

Daddy often boasted about being a member of the illustrious "Hell Hole Swamp Gang," which consisted of native sons of Berkeley County who went on to gain political prominence in South Carolina—Governor Robert E. McNair, S.C. State Senator Rembert Dennis and Columbia Mayor Lester Bates being the other members of the "gang."

It was in the fall of 1965 that Daddy was again uniquely honored when the North Charleston Kiwanis Club had a bronze bust of him erected in front of a library building on Rivers Avenue. The club had mounted a year-long fund-raising drive during which it received both large and small donations for the project.

It was a rainy, gusty day and a small tent had to be put up at the last minute over the speakers' platform. It was one of those days when no one wanted to venture out, but many had. Mother unveiled the bust, an excellent likeness of Daddy done by Arthur Bruce Hoheb of New York, while someone held an umbrella over her head.

Daddy knew when to be brief in his remarks. Several speakers praised him before he had a chance to speak: "I would be foolish to attempt to make a speech after these tributes have been heaped on such unworthy shoulders. I would not wish to impose upon you, who have sat through this rain to attend this honor for me.

"A man does not seek public office for glory. If glory results from a man's career, it usually comes after his death. That I should receive this sign of the love of the people of my home while living makes me very happy and proud indeed."

Earlier that year Daddy had become Chairman of the Armed Services Committee and the top brass had turned out for him on that rainy day. The Secretaries of the Army, Navy, and Air Force were there, as was the head of the CIA, several Admirals, Generals and Congressmen.

A Columbia newspaper printed a tongue-in-cheek memo about the many high-ranking dignitaries attending: "Secretaries of the Navy and

Air Force will head a list of dignitaries in Charleston for the unveiling of
a monument to U.S. Rep. L. Mendel Rivers.

> To: High-Ranking Pentagon Personnel
> From: Secretary of Defense
> This is an order, fellas, so
> Let's not hear any wailing:
> You'll all get down to Charleston
> For Mendel's big unveiling.
> He holds the purse strings, so attend
> E'en though you didn't plan it.
> Though he's immortalized in stone,
> We can't take him for granite.
>
> (Submitted by Jolly Jim)

Daddy was particularly proud to receive honorary degrees from
three South Carolina colleges—The Citadel, Clemson University and
the College of Charleston—and from Sheldon College in New Jersey.

The College of Charleston meant a great deal to Daddy, probably as
much from a loyalty point of view as from the institution's value to the
community.

Former College President Theodore Stern told me that when he
was about to retire from the Navy that Daddy called him at the Naval
Supply Center in Charleston, which he had commanded for several
years: "Ted, we want you to be president of the College of Charleston."
Ted thanked him but said that he had been offered the position of
Deputy Controller General of the U.S., and that among other attractive
aspects to the job, meant a salary far greater than what a small college
president was paid. "Ted," continued Daddy, "you do know that the
Congress has to approve the appointment of the Deputy Controller
General, don't you?"

"Yes, I know that," answered Ted, demurring slightly. "And just
when would the job with the college begin?"

"September the first," Daddy said.

"But this is August 24. I can't retire from the Navy and get everything all straightened out in only a week."

"You certainly can." Within 48 hours Ted had his retirement papers, pay and all, in his hands, and he did become the strong, new president of the College of Charleston—and a tireless community leader.

Within a couple of years there was a strong movement to make the College a part of the state's system of higher education. Firmly against it, however, was the powerful Speaker of the S.C. House of Representatives, Solomon Blatt. Daddy, Joe Riley and Ted Stern visited Speaker Blatt at his home in the town of Barnwell.

The story goes that Blatt later recounted the visit: "That Mendel Rivers, that Joe Riley and that Ted Stern came to my house. I was unalterably opposed to the College of Charleston coming into the state system. They drank my liquor, they ate my food and by the time the evening was over, I was the strongest supporter of the College coming in..."

Joe Riley, Jr., who would later serve as Charleston's Mayor, was then a State Representative and introduced the legislation regarding the College of Charleston in March of 1970. Daddy went to Columbia for the vote, and sat on the dais next to the Speaker and watched as the bill was given unanimous approval.

My father saw his name put on many things in Charleston while he was alive, including the L. Mendel Rivers Federal Building, a military housing project called MenRiv Park, Rivers Gate at the Charleston Air Force Base, and the main Post Office facility (Rivers Annex) in North Charleston.

In October of 1970, the L. Mendel Rivers Library was dedicated at the Baptist College at Charleston (now Charleston Southern University). A long-time supporter of the college's efforts to get established and a friend of its president, the Reverend John Hamrick, my father was deeply honored by the gesture. Even though the skies promised, not merely threatened, severe showers, 8,000 people came to the dedication ceremonies. Al Hirt, the famed trumpet player, played the national anthem. The Reverend Billy Graham was the main speaker for the day. "It never rains when Billy Graham speaks," Daddy predicted as he introduced the evangelist. With near-perfect timing, however, as Dr. Graham stood up to give his remarks, the heavens opened up. "Well, I can tell you one thing about Mendel Rivers," he said to the crowd. "He certainly is no prophet..."

After his death, his portrait was hung in the South Carolina State House, the plaza fronting the Charleston Naval Hospital was named for him and two rooms on the *U. S. S. Yorktown* in Charleston harbor (a naval museum) were named for him. Within a few years of his death, a committee of his friends and supporters had raised money to have a bust cast and a small park created in his honor next to the County Courthouse in downtown Charleston. Numerous chapters of military organizations both in his district and elsewhere have been named in his honor. More than 15 years after his death, the Army recruit processing center at Fort Jackson in Columbia was named for him, and a VIP visitors suite and the tactical command building at Shaw Air Force Base in Sumter bore his name.

CHAPTER 9

If the assassination of President Kennedy had not been enough, the political atmosphere in America, unfortunately, became frightening as the 1960s progressed. It would get worse and worse as the decade drew to a close.

When Lyndon Johnson and Barry Goldwater ran for the office of President in 1964, the heated campaigns of both candidates caused great excitement all over the country.

Nowhere was the election a more volatile issue than in Daddy's own backyard. The South was clearly a region that had to be courted by the Democrats. Among other things, South Carolina's Senator Strom Thurmond had just switched party labels and gone over to the Republican side. (Senator Thurmond told me that Daddy was one of the few who encouraged him to change to the Republican Party and follow the dictates of his conscience: "Mendel encouraged me by telling me to do what I thought was the right thing to do.")

Daddy was among those whom the Democratic Party expected to help in the effort to win the election.

In South Carolina some of the biggest commotion was generated by the visit of the Lady Bird Special, the First Lady's whistle stop train tour through eight Southern states. Even before the tour began in Alexandria, Virginia, it promised to be a bumpy ride for Mrs. Johnson as she ventured into an area that loudly proclaimed itself to be for Barry Goldwater. The train was patriotically dressed out in red, white and blue bunting. The stops it made employed all the razzle-dazzle familiar in political campaigns. Mrs. Johnson and her daughters, Lynda Bird, 20, and Luci, 17, addressed the gathered crowds from the train's rear platform at numerous places along the route. A contingent of "Johnson Girls," brightly costumed, appeared with the party to lend enthusiasm and festivity at each stop. Bands played and Democrats cheered. Local Democratic leaders boarded the train at the whistle stops to praise the Johnson-Humphrey team and to urge voters to cast their ballots for the Democratic ticket in the upcoming election.

Lady Bird Johnson was in many ways breaking new ground in campaigning. Her tour and public speeches on behalf of her husband were considered by many to be behavior unbecoming to the First Lady of the United States. Political wives in the past, were supposed to be with their husbands on the campaign trail if deemed necessary for the effort—but not as active campaigners and certainly not on their own. Unfortunately, the reception that the First Lady received was not always warm.

Excitement intensified in Charleston the day before the arrival of the train when reports of the First Lady's appearance in the state capital of Columbia reached Charleston. When Mrs. Johnson had attempted to speak to her audience, a crowd of rowdy young Goldwater fans had continuously interrupted and harassed her. An embarrassed Governor Donald Russell had made efforts to silence the demonstrators, but with little success. The First Lady had determinedly delivered her speech, saying, "This is a country of many viewpoints. I respect your rights to express yours. Now, it's my turn to express mine."

Except for a few Goldwater placards here and there, it was the first time that any organized opposition had met the train on its route through the South.

An LBJ Rally was held for Mrs. Johnson at the new Pinehaven Shopping Center on Rivers Avenue when the train reached Charleston. Various singing groups entertained the crowd while Charleston officials met the train to escort Lady Bird and her entourage of nineteen cars to the Pinehaven Center. Although extra security forces had been provided, many feared that violence would break out in the noisy gathering, which was estimated at between 10,000 and 20,000 people.

When Lady Bird, carrying a large bouquet of yellow roses, began to mount the steps of the speakers' platform, a loud chanting of "We Want Barry" broke out from a group of young people who waved Goldwater signs. Calm and poised, Mrs. Johnson was ushered to the front row of the platform where she was seated between Daddy and her two daughters.

When Daddy introduced Mrs. Johnson, he shocked some of his Goldwater constituents. "I'm gonna tell you something you can't read in the newspapers. I have come here tonight to tell you why I don't plan to leave the Democratic party, and I have not come here to apologize for being a Democrat."

Referring to his support for Eisenhower in 1952, Daddy reminded his audience of some of the realities of the world of politics: "I tried one time. I tried a man named Dwight Eisenhower...The next thing I knew Fort Jackson was to be closed, the Navy Yard non-existent, and the Air Base was to be skeletonized. I got a belly full of Dwight Eisenhower...I didn't apologize when I got the Veterans Administration Hospital here that was not slated to be here. I didn't apologize when I got the Polaris base. I didn't apologize for the Polaris fleet—two fleets, 20,000 personnel."

And of the hecklers, he said: "I don't know who these people are, but they are not the high class people I know who think they support Goldwater. Whoever is responsible should be ashamed of himself if he knows what manners are."

Mrs. Johnson's address touched on several subjects. She praised Charleston for its roots in the traditions and beauties of the past, as well as its will to move forward into the future. "This is what makes Charleston such an exciting city...Just as Charleston has been the watchdog of the Atlantic, my husband, with Mendel Rivers, served as watch dog of our defenses." She applauded her husband's record and appealed for a governmental partnership that would mean "jobs and a better community to live in." And she gently reminded her audience that a Democratic victory would mean that Mendel Rivers would become the Chairman of the Armed Services Committee of the House.

The chanting for Goldwater was almost constant, but Mrs. Johnson received frequent applause throughout the evening. Several people on the speakers' stand were openly critical of the hecklers. Lt. Governor Robert E. McNair said, "I never thought I would have to apologize for anybody in South Carolina."

Mrs. Olin Johnston, wife of the South Carolina Senator, had only one thing to say when she got up to speak: "That crowd over there is scared to death or they wouldn't be acting like such idiots."

Hale Boggs, Congressman from Louisiana and the Democratic Whip in the House, who was travelling with the First Lady, was even stronger. "I notice," he said, "there are some young people here who have no sense of American democracy...This is an American gathering and not a Nazi gathering." Attempting to shout above the noise of the crowd, he declared Goldwater would not carry South Carolina in the election "and one of the reasons...is because of Mendel Rivers."

Early the next morning, Daddy and Mayor Palmer Gaillard met Mrs. Johnson to escort her on a tour of historic sights in downtown Charleston. They rode in an antique horse-drawn open carriage through the old streets of the city, making several stops.

After the carriage tour, Mother joined Mrs. Johnson and Daddy for a continuation of sightseeing in a car conspicuously marked "The First Lady." Mother gave her a copy of the popular Junior League cookbook *Charleston Receipts* as a reminder of her visit. Although Mother was a secret supporter of Goldwater, she was somewhat embarrassed along their route to see her nephews among a group of young school children holding up Goldwater signs. "I couldn't pretend indignation when I was in sympathy with the demonstrators," Mother said, "but I know that it must have been painful for Mrs. Johnson."

Palmer Gaillard told me that the visit to Charleston by Lady Bird Johnson had been difficult for many Charlestonians, politicians in particular, because of the strong Goldwater support in the area. "Mendel and I were both in a tough situation...We had an obligation to the country to welcome Mrs. Johnson, the First Lady, not merely a candidate's wife. It was our responsibility to do so."

On the way back to the train station, Daddy showed Mrs. Johnson the Four Mile House. He told her the story of the beautiful Lavinia

Fisher who had lived there when it had been an inn in the early nine-teenth century. She and her husband had robbed and murdered many unsuspecting travellers after rigging up a trap door through which the victims fell to their deaths. They were finally convicted of their crimes and sentenced to a public hanging. The prosecutor was Robert Hayne, who was to be Daniel Webster's opponent in the "Great Debate" of 1830. The story was that Lavinia yelled to the crowd assembled to watch her hanging: "If you have a message you want to send to Hell, give it to me—I'll carry it."

Mrs. Johnson was so impressed by the story that she remembered it in detail and mentioned it to Daddy several years later.

After the visit of the Lady Bird Special, many Goldwater supporters among Daddy's constituents were disappointed in him and several news-paper editorials and letters-to-the-editor expressed indignation. He was accused of having adopted a pork barrel attitude towards politics and of having grovelled at Johnson's feet.

Among those who came to his defense was Frank Gilbreath in his popular column "Ashley Cooper: Doing the Charleston":

"I wish that the Goldwaterites would stop teasing Rep. L. Mendel Rivers, simply because he was on the Lady Bird Special when it came to North Charleston.

"Although Mendel occasionally may be guilty of playing the 'see-what-I-got-for-you' game in politics, he has been (and in this paragraph I am dead serious) a splendid representative, not only for the First Congressional district, but for the country as a whole. He is a patriot, an able politician and a credit to the Holy City.

"Yes, a good many of the very people who are now teasing Mendel would have a duck fit and start screaming abuses if Mendel should announce tomorrow that he is a Republican—and thus lose the chair-manship of the Armed Services Committee, which will mean so much to Charleston.

"So you all quit kidding Mendel-Bird—Whoops! I mean Rep. Rivers—hear?"

Another writer, Roulac Hamilton, said in his "Dateline Washington" column:

Old Democratic friends John F. Kennnedy, Mendel Rivers and Lyndon Johnson in the fall of 1960.

My father encouraged Billy Graham to speak to the corps of cadets at The Citadel. From left: Mendel Rivers, Renie Clark, Billy Graham and General Mark W. Clark, president of The Citadel.

In the late 1960s, there was much talk about long hair among the younger generation. It did not affect the hair styles of at least two Congressmen— from left: House Speaker John McCormack, Mendel Rivers, Gerald Ford and Leslie Arends. (Democratic National Congressional Committee, Dev O'Neill, Committee Photographer)

Lady Bird Johnson waving a greeting upon her arrival in Charleston on the Lady Bird Special, a train touring the southeastern U.S. in the election of 1964. My father was her host on this visit, seen here with her daughter Lynda. (Charleston *News & Courier* photograph).

The new House Armed Services Committee room was named for longtime former chairman Carl Vinson of Georgia, seen here receiving congratulations from President Lyndon Johnson in 1965. The new chairman, Mendel Rivers, holds the name sign from behind the podium.

President Johnson gives one of the pens used to sign legislation into law to its author, Mendel Rivers, October 1965.

Mendel Rivers and Lyndon Johnson understood each other and were sometimes political allies and sometimes foes. They are seen here in 1966. Deputy Secretary of Defense Cyrus Vance observes.

Former President Dwight Eisenhower paid the new Armed Services Committee chairman a visit in 1965.

Chairman Rivers and General William Westmoreland, 1968. (Photograph by SSG Wayne Vernon, U.S. Army Signal Support Unit, MDW)

My father congratulates General Daniel "Chappie" James, the first black to attain that rank in the Air Force, 1968. After my father's death, Gen. James wrote my mother that he "lost my best friend." (Democratic National Congressional Committee, Dev O'Neill, Committee Photographer)

In 1964, my father escorts me during a festivity in the annual Cherry Blossom Festival in Washington where I represented South Carolina.

Chairman of the House Armed Services Committee Carl Vinson, Secretary of Defense Robert S. McNamara and committee member Mendel Rivers, 1963.

My father greets soldiers during a visit to South Korea in 1965.

Mendel Rivers greets Generalissimo Chaing Kai-shek in Taiwan in 1965. (Photo by Wu Chung Yee)

Shortly after becoming Chairman of the Armed Services Committee, my father went to Vietnam, seen here on arrival with General William Westmoreland. (Photograph by SSGT. K. W. Kelley, U.S. Marine Corps.)

Congressman Rivers talking with constituents.

My father hosted a luncheon on Capital Hill for Madame Chaing Kai-shek when she visited Washington in 1968.

Coralee Bull of Beaufort, South Carolina, served for many years as my father's administrative assistant. (Democratic National Congressional Committee, Dev O'Neill, Committee Photographer)

Boxer Jack Dempsey (left) and World War II flying hero Roland Wooten of South Carolina (center) became friends when they travelled together to sell war bonds, seen here with my father in 1967.

"The Father of the Nuclear Navy," Admiral Hyman Rickover with my father on a visit to the Charleston Navy Yard in 1968. (U.S. Navy Photograph).

In 1969 when I was in Europe, my father invited me to join him when he attended the NATO Assembly meeting in Brussels. Another Congressional delegate was Sen. Edward Kennedy (right) Mrs. Kennedy is opposite her husband.

This is one of my favorite photographs of my father and me, taken in 1969.

My father holds a youngster in front of the newly-renamed Rivers Elementary School in Altus, Oklahoma. He authored legislation which put an Air Force training school at the small base near the town in 1970. (Democratic National Congressional Committee, Dev O'Neill, Committee Photographer)

Frank Jameson and my father at the unveiling ceremony in 1968. The portrait hangs in the House Armed Services Committee hearing room.

A letter from Richard Nixon, December 28, 1970.

Pictured at the keel laying ceremonies for the *U.S.S. L. Mendel Rivers* in June, 1971, are (left to right) Congressman F. Edward Hébert, chairman of the House Armed Services Committee, Mrs. Mendel Rivers, Secretary of the Navy Chafee, Mrs. Hébert and Admiral Elmo Zumwalt.

My sister, Peg Eastman (left) and I christen the *U.S.S. L. Mendel Rivers* in 1973.

The *U.S.S. L. Mendel Rivers* slides off the drydock at the christening ceremonies to the strains of *Anchors Away*. God Speed.

"That 'politics makes strange bedfellows' is an ancient truism, and perhaps the adage never has been better proven than by Rep. L. Mendel Rivers' seemingly enthusiastic support for the Johnson-Humphrey ticket.

"Anyone who has followed the career of the Charleston Congressman must be fully aware that he not only is no left-winger, but that he also is not given to the blind kind of partisanship which calls for support of Democratic administration policies when they offend his conscience or the way of life of his constituency.

"...But Rivers knows the man in the White House...And he knows, although he cannot say so, that the man in the White House is fully capable of using his influence to strip any Democrat in the House who opposes him—for that matter, who does not actively support him—of committee chairmanships, and even party privileges and seniority. And he knows also that the man in the White House can end any federal build-up of a district represented by an opposing Congressman."

Within two months, Daddy was sworn in as Chairman of the House Armed Services Committee.

Mrs. Johnson wrote to Daddy when she got back to Washington at the end of the Lady Bird Special tour of the South: "Dear Mendel: Thank you for your letter of the 21st and for being on the train with me. The more I learned about the political climate of your area, the more I understood it took courage and strong friendship. I appreciate it and I realize what it meant for us to have you aboard...I have already very hurriedly written you to thank you for the *Charleston Receipts*, but that was at a time before I have really sat down to convey my *real feelings* to those who contributed so much..." Lyndon and I send our best to you and Margaret."

A couple of years later, probably for the first time in his life, Daddy ran out of gas driving along the George Washington Parkway on his way home. He pushed his car up off the road, wondering what would be the best thing to do next, when a chauffeured limousine stopped suddenly and backed up to where he stood. It was Lady Bird Johnson, who gave him a ride home.

Daddy and Mother were invited to several dinner parties at the

White House, and sometimes were received beforehand in the Johnsons' private quarters for refreshments and conversation. On one occasion, the President announced to Daddy: "Oh, Mendel! I brought you something from my last trip..." and he left the room and returned with a handsome necktie.

Daddy and Lyndon Johnson had served together in the House in the 1940s and on the same committee. They had plenty of disagreements, particularly after Daddy became Chairman, but they knew how to get along with each other. They could good-naturedly banter back and forth. Members of Daddy's staff recalled that Daddy occasionally refused calls from a White House "underling," and insisted that he would only talk to the President himself on the issue in question. In conversation, he would call him "Lyndon" rather than "Mr. President" at times.

One time Daddy left the office early and gave his office staff strict instructions not to give *anyone* his home telephone number, which was unlisted. Coralee Bull, Daddy's Administrative Assistant, had to tell the President of the United States that she could not give out Mr. Rivers' home phone number. The next day Daddy told her that President Johnson had managed to find out his number and had called him on an important matter, adding, "Mrs. Bull, there are *some* people you may give my number to..."

Daddy genuinely liked Mrs. Johnson and it was easy to see why. She was a poised and courteous lady. On the one occasion when I met her, at a large Democratic function, she was warm and friendly, and had the gift and ability to make each individual guest feel at ease with her. I was impressed. My mother was with her many times and told me: "I admired Lady Bird even though I didn't share her political views. After all, it must be a quantum leap to become First Lady of the land, one that requires tremendous stamina and adaptability. I felt that she did it gracefully."

CHAPTER 10

When Mendel Rivers picked up the gavel as the new Chairman of the House Armed Services Committee in January of 1965, he left little doubt as to how he viewed his new role and that of his committee.

And just in case anyone else might be in doubt, a gleaming, new plaque appeared on the front of the dais in the committee hearing room where he presided:

> U.S. Constitution — Art. 1 — Sec. 8
> The Congress shall have Power...
> To raise and support Armies...
> provide and maintain a Navy...
> make Rules for the Government and
> Regulation of the land and naval forces.

The inscription, permanently etched in bronze, measured two feet across and nearly two feet high and faced every witness, friendly and hostile, testifying before the committee.

The military had known for years that it had a friend in Congress. Throughout his career in Congress, he had taken on various fights on behalf of the defense structure of the country. It was pretty cut and dry for Mendel Rivers. His country's military had to be Number One: "...second best in this business means being last." Its champion was now in a powerful enough position to make a real difference.

He had never served one day in the armed forces, which, he told one reporter, was his "deepest regret...I am a member of that lost, in-between generation. I was 12 years old when World War I broke out, and I was too old for World War II." In a way, I think, he felt a little guilty that he hadn't served in the military. But he frequently pointed out why he supported the armed services so strongly: "Why, *all* the military has ever done for me is protect me and my country in three wars in my lifetime." He might not have been in uniform, but he never stopped thanking and applauding those who were.

Literally hundreds of legislative bills designed to make life even a little better for the servicemen had his name on them. Most of these pieces of legislation were not the headline-catching glamour issues. They did not necessarily win him any votes at home and they were not especially high-profile. During his early years in Congress, for example, he became an advocate of upgrading dentists serving in the armed forces to the ranks held by physicians in the medical corps—a battle which he ultimately won and which earned him lasting appreciation from dentists, both military and civilian. Military housing, medical care for dependents, and retirement benefits were vital pieces of legislation for him.

One high-ranking Admiral once told Daddy's successor in Congress: "Mendel Rivers ruined the God-damned Navy giving these men higher wages and houses to live in so they could get married. We never could keep them on the ships again."

Daddy could discuss with military professionals the in-depth, minute details of the manufacture and operation of airplanes, tanks, guns and submarines. He had an exceptional retention ability and could recall statistics on just about every aspect of military life. It could never be said that he didn't do his homework.

"Our military personnel cannot lobby...They cannot go on strike...In short, once committed to a military career, these personnel can look only to Congress," Daddy had once pointed out. "It's my job to know everything there is to know about the military."

He took on his job with a seriousness that was to be admired. As Chairman, he was treated like a reigning monarch by all military personnel, enlisted and officer alike. He was clearly a hero.

"Mr. Rivers usually received what he asked for from the military," Coralee Bull told me, tongue-in-cheek. "The Army and Air Force *never* turned down a request, the Navy seldom. The Marines *might* say No, but sent over two 2-Star Generals with the personal message."

His military pay bills probably earned him the most recognition. He was frequently at odds with the Administration, be it Democrat or Republican, over many benefits for the military, especially concerning pay increases. While the civilian sector of federal employees regularly received pay increases, the military did not, and Daddy kept up the fight to better balance that lopsided situation. It was not something that he felt required any discussion and compromise whatsover, but merely that "the soldier should enjoy the same standard of living as that which he is defending—nothing less."

Retired Navy captain Theodore S. Stern told me: "He worked for all of us, but the lower the rank, the harder Mendel fought."

In 1965, my father authored a pay raise bill that gave the lower ranks of enlisted men the first pay increase that they had received since 1952! The bill passed the House of Representatives by a vote of 410-0. (He was made an "Honorary Officer" and disbursed one of the first checks reflecting the pay raise.)

Members of his office staff said that on many, many occasions he would interrupt his schedule to talk with young enlisted men who would come to his office without an appointment. "He would stop everything," Kathy Worthington told me, "and talk to the G.I., take him on a tour of the office and ask him about life in the service."

I have been told that Daddy once kept Generals and Colonels waiting, while on an inspection trip in West Germany, while he chatted with young airmen. My brother was with my father one time when he went 50 miles out of his way to give a lift to two hitch-hiking sailors.

He thrived on the praise and the power. He loved it.

The Armed Services Committee Room is large, impressive and rather awe-inspiring. It is decorated in blue with heavy velvet curtains hanging at the tall windows, a carpet with federal motifs in the design and military flags complete with battle streamers displayed. The room is located near the main entrance at the top of a long circular driveway of the Rayburn House Office Building. Shortly after the opening of Congress in 1965, the room was named the Carl Vinson Room in honor of the former Chairman who had served for so many years and had recently retired from Congress.

Vinson came up from Georgia for the ceremonies. President Lyndon Johnson also came, on Daddy's invitation, from 1600 Pennsylvania Avenue, to pay his respects as Commander in Chief to the committee members responsible for the armed services.

There were 40 members of the Committee and the Resident Commissioner from Puerto Rico. Daddy, from the very beginning, sought to have his committee work together, not on a partisan basis. It was not always an easy job.

Russ Blandford, the Chief Counsel of the Committee, accompanied Daddy when he first inspected the new committee room and staff offices.

"Russ, what are those two rooms?" he inquired, referring to two small anterooms on opposite sides of the main hearing room.

"Mr. Chairman, one room is a caucus room for the Democrats and the other is for the Republicans," he answered. (All hearing rooms in the building were of that design.)

Russ said that he remembered that Daddy had fire in his eyes when he said: "We aren't going to have Democrats and Republicans on my committee, only Americans. Lock one of them, or make it an office for someone. There'll be no party caucusing."

Russ, a former military man who viewed national defense pretty much the way his boss did, was impresssed. He recounted this story many times. "It was not a publicity stunt. There was no one else around."

Within several months, Daddy, inevitably, started rescheduling his committee meetings earlier and earlier, sometimes at 7:00 a.m. He was a stickler for knowing the rules by which his committee and the Congress worked. He knew how to use those rules with confidence, and especially wanted the committee to work as one under his leadership. Daddy was determined to bring all of the committee members, including freshmen, into the deliberations. While there was no denying Chairman Vinson's abilities or his vast knowledge of military affairs, he had "ruled" autocratically and often did not consult other members of the committee on many issues. One committee member, Porter Hardy of Virginia, said of Daddy after he had been Chairman for several months: "Times are considerably different from what they were under Mr. Vinson. A main difference is in the extent to which Mendel takes the members into his confidence and keeps them informed. Mr. Vinson didn't do much of that."

Vinson of Georgia had served in Congress for a half century, and had left an indelible mark on the committee for which he had served as Chairman. According to what some said about Mr. Vinson after his retirement in 1964, he was an extremely astute politician in a subtle sort of way, who quietly but effectively got his legislation passed without having to resort to open partisan battles. He rarely, if ever, had any political opposition for re-election to Congress in his district in Milledgeville, representing it continuously after being elected in 1914 (when Daddy was nine years old). In 1931, he became chairman of the Naval Affairs Committee and then of the Armed Services Committee when the committee structures were reorganized after World War II.

From what I understand, Mr. Vinson had his own "style" in dealing with committee members, as well as the Administration and those in the military. He, said many who had worked with him, liked to work somewhat on his own or with a small, select group of the full committee.

Mr. Vinson, because of his assured position in Congress, did not fully appreciate the need by other members of his committee, or any Members of Congress for that matter, to actively campaign for re-election. He had never had to do much more than just pay his filing fee. He felt that anyone who had to raise money to be re-elected was virtually being bought. Most Members of Congress needed to spend time in their districts to gain the necessary exposure among constituents making speeches, shaking hands and raising money for campaign expenses.

He expected all of the Armed Services Committee members, though, to follow his example and to remain in Washington until the end of each week although most Congressional business generally slowed down on Fridays mainly so that Congressmen *could* spend weekends in their districts.

Coralee Bull told me that on one occasion Daddy left for

Charleston by mid-afternoon on a Thursday, departing with the instruction: "Don't let Vinson know." By the end of the day, she had not heard from Mr. Vinson's office and sighed a sigh of relief as she left for the evening. When the elevator door opened, there stood Mr. Vinson. Caught off-guard, she muttered something about some forgotten papers in her office, stepped back and watched the elevator doors close. For some 15 minutes, she avoided taking that elevator. When she finally did, convinced she could not possibly run into the committee chairman again, the elevator doors opened and there stood Carl Vinson.

In 1959, Daddy was named by Chairman Vinson to head Subcommittee Number 3 of the Armed Services Committee, one of four numbered committees, thus becoming a member of Vinson's inner policy-making circle. Daddy no longer sat on any other standing House committees and concentrated on learning and refining his knowledge about all aspects of the military and defense. Daddy was frequently sent by Mr. Vinson, who did not enjoy travelling, on fact-finding missions and military inspection trips to various places in this country and abroad.

Daddy became the ranking Democratic member of the Committee in 1961, upon the resignation of Congressman Paul Kilday of Texas who was appointed to serve as judge of the U.S. Court of Military Appeals. As ranking member, his voice carried more weight, of course, in Congress. He was given more and more responsibility by Chairman Vinson, who was expected to announce his retirement at any time.

By the time "Uncle Carl" (as he was affectionately called) retired at the age of 80, he and Daddy had worked closely together for nearly a quarter of a century, and had gotten along well. They were both early risers and often ate breakfast together in the House Office Building Cafeteria.

After so many years in Congress and as Chairman of the Committee, Vinson, quite understandably, felt very protective about the Committee and its leadership after leaving Capitol Hill. Shortly before his retirement, he remarked to Daddy that upon becoming Chairman he would see things differently: "As Chairman one's perspective suddenly becomes infinitely more national and international and less local and regional in scope; the responsibilities would become far more burden-some." Daddy often referred to having been "schooled" by Carl Vinson, and gave him a great deal of the credit for his outlooks on military affairs. They sometimes approached things differently, but they shared the same view of a strong and ready national defense.

Daddy quickly established his own mark on the committee, which, undoubtedly, was one of the most influential committees in the Congress. The Armed Services Committee of the House, when Daddy became Chairman, handled legislation for some $80 billion in spending.

Mendel Rivers, reported *Esquire* magazine, went from obscurity to being a powerful Congressman when he became the Chairman of the committee: "Rivers is the American who, in the name of Congress and with the authority of the Constitution, raises armies and launches navies. After the President, he may be the most powerful man in the country..."

As the new Chairman, he was to have plenty of critics as well as sup-porters. He did not always have the full support of all of the committee members as much as he tried to garner it. One small group on the com-mittee became known as the "Fearless Five." When not in agreement with the majority of the committee members—including the chair-man—on specific issues, these members complained that they were denied key subcommittee assignments because of it.

One of Daddy's sharpest critics, Otis Pike of New York, claimed that Daddy was "a master of the carrot and stick tactic," who would reward members who stood with him: "Ours is a difference in philosophy. Mendel cannot understand why if he treats me well in committee I feel free to go out and oppose him on the Floor. He believes the committee should close ranks after it has voted."

"It's awfully hard to dislike Mendel," he added to a reporter doing a profile on Daddy. "I don't see how you can...Anyone who thinks he is a fool is himself an idiot."

After Daddy's death, Congressman Pike said of him: "He had a magnificent sense of humor, and while he could use it devastatingly in debate, and frequently used it against me, he could also laugh at him-self...His judgements were not always my judgements and his priorities were not always mine. I frequently questioned his judgements and his priorities. But I have never questioned his motives."

Another rebel on his committee, Robert Leggett of California, took issue with Daddy's preferences in spending, fearing too much of the budget was going to defense programs while too little was designated for domestic agendas. He said, however, that he felt that Daddy sincerely believed that what he was advocating was right: "The chairman honestly believes $82 billion is not too much for the military. At the same time, he...will not support social programs which I, as a liberal, think we've got to have if we are to survive...I don't oppose him out of obstinacy."

When Daddy was criticized in the press for the number of military installations in his district, Leggett came to his defense: "When they try to tie the can to him for what he's done for his district, I don't go along. Maybe I'm schizophrenic. I have a half-billion dollar military payroll in my district."

Daddy was sometimes accused of giving things to the military even when they didn't want them. He was no pushover, though, one military writer once said in his defense, and did not want *anyone* to play around with the taxpayers' money. "I've had a lot of *unpleasant* experiences with the military," Daddy once said. "I've opposed them on many issues, and I've had so much grief over officers coming before my committee with a bunch of bum dope that I've had to develop a basic skepticism about the testimony we get."

There were many critics who opposed Daddy's pro-military stance and the large price tag attached to it, but he once said of them: "My critics, who are legion, will attempt to dismiss what I say...by categorizing [it] as the shrill cries of a hawk who is suffering the agonies of reduced defense expenditures...If this occurs, I will have failed my purpose since I believe that these critics, who love America no less than I, will, if they assess my words carefully, find that we not only have a common concern, but a common and frightening peril."

He was successful in getting his bills passed in Congress for many reasons (and his success rate was phenomenal) besides his dedication.

"...Rivers holds the all-time won-and-lost record...Rivers never lost a bill in committee or on the floor, an accomplishment, he noted one day, that even 'Caesar in all his glory' couldn't equal," said Daniel Rapoport in his book, *Inside the House*. Rapoport, a United Press International reporter who covered the House of Representatives for many years, also seemed to feel that my father's record of accomplishment was due in part to his overbearing attitude. "Rivers brooded a lot, stormed around, chewed out people and generally took himself and his responsibilities very seriously....[He] had triggered angry outbursts on several occasions when he arbitrarily decided that there had been enough talk on a bill or amendment and rallied a majority to cut off further debate."

Strom Thurmond said that he, as the ranking Republican on the Senate Armed Services Committee, worked many times with Daddy in conference committees to iron differences between House and Senate versions of legislation. "You have to have support in *both* bodies of Congress to get legislation passed. Mendel had a dominant personality that allowed him to get a lot of things done that other people could not. I always respected him because he was so decisive. He reminded me of a general in the Army or Air Force or of an admiral in the Navy because they have to be able to make decisions promptly and do it firmly without equivocation. That's the way Mendel was.

"He was the kind of fellow you could put your finger on, be sure of. You didn't have to go back to him over and over. If he told you he was going to do something, he'd do it. You could go to sleep on what Mendel Rivers told you."

He knew instinctively how to get along even with those with whom he strongly disagreed. And he genuinely liked people. Once I was having lunch with Daddy in the Capitol Dining Room and he introduced me to a young Congressman from New York, Allard Lowenstein. He was a liberal New Yorker who for years had worked within the system of the Democratic Party to change America's political direction. He vehemently opposed my father on just about every issue, particularly Vietnam. I was surprised that my father had been particularly friendly to this "enemy." But he reminded me that "you don't have to be disagreeable to disagree. He's a bright young man and I can understand his point of view."

Lowenstein and my father were odd bedfellows indeed. I remember reading a story about Lowenstein's wife watching him talking with my father on the Floor of the House while she observed from the Visitors' Gallery. Later, she asked about the conversation, questioning why Mr. Rivers had held up several fingers while talking with him. "Was he telling you just how long you would last in Congress? Just a few years?," she inquired. "No," Lowenstein replied, "he was telling me about the long-standing Jewish community in Charleston and about the number of synagogues there."

In his book, *The Pied Piper*, Richard Cummings said that "Congressmen who had expected Lowenstein to behave like a wild-eyed radical were won over. The Chairman of the House Armed Services Committee, Mendel Rivers of South Carolina, with whom Lowenstein clashed on the floor of the House, came to respect him, particularly as he became aware of Lowenstein's anti-Communism...Lowenstein's efforts to become part of the 'club' in Congress took some bizarre twists. With Mendel Rivers, he co-chaired a luncheon for Zbigniew Stypulkowski, the last 'ambassador' of Free Poland before the U.S. recognized the Communist regime...During the first months of his term, Lowenstein was taken aside by Rivers, an old-fashioned Southern conservative, and told: 'Lowenstein, my boy, you and I may not see eye to eye on lots of things. But I like you and when you run for re-election, I will come and campaign for you, or against you, whichever you want.'"

After Senator Edward Kennedy's tragic mishandling of the Chappaquidick incident, Daddy rose above his political differences with him with a small gesture of kindness; Daddy sent several pounds of South Carolina shrimp to the Senator's office with a note of sympathy.

A *Wall Street Journal* article once quoted a "Northern Democratic liberal": "When I first came to Congress I despised Mendel Rivers and everything he stood for, but after seeing what an indefatigable worker he is and experiencing his personal warmth, I've become very sympathetic toward him."

Daddy also had a good sense of humor, an essential ingredient, I would think, for survival in the public light. During a debate on the defense structure sponsored by the Foreign Relations Council at the

University of Southern California, he drew a laugh from the audience when he quipped: "I happen to know about losing wars. I come from a part of the country where we lost a war, and I don't intend to let that happen again."

Another time, after delivering a speech before a college student gathering, a member of the audience came up to him and told him that he had misquoted Abraham Lincoln. "Well," responded Daddy, "if he didn't say it, he should have."

He could lash back at opponents with a piercing retort, with effective and masterful use of language. One of his favorites was: "...He disturbs the even surface of my mood more lightly than the tilted swallow's wings disturbs the limpid, glassy solitude of the sound, clear pool."

The new Rayburn House Office Building was completed in time for the new Congress convening in January, 1965. For all the criticism of the building both then and now, it has many advantages over the Cannon and Longworth Buildings, and it contains the offices of choice for most Congressmen. A few months prior to his becoming Chairman, Daddy and Mother, along with dozens of other Congressmen, wives and staff members, had scurried around the Rayburn Building to select a suite of offices.

The one they finally settled on seemed ideal for Daddy: it was a couple of stories above street level, affording privacy and security; convenient to the Armed Services Committee Room; and probably had the most outstanding view of the Capitol Dome available. Mother could say with pride that the selection of Room 2205 was initially hers. She realized what a good choice she had made when, after Daddy died, she was given only a short time to vacate the offices because the Speaker of the House, Carl Albert, wanted the office for himself.

The rules of the House of Representatives stipulate that when a Congressman dies in office, his staff has to give up the offices he occupied upon request of the next member on the seniority list. "Rivers' suite on the second floor of the Rayburn Building," reported one newspaper, "was considered a plum. The congressman's office had an excellent view of the Capitol...Newly elected Speaker of the House Carl Albert of Oklahoma wasted little time in claiming the quarters. Rivers' staff was given two rather small rooms in the Longworth building."

Daddy commuted from a home he had recently purchased in McLean, Virginia, located just off the George Washington Parkway. It was an unpretentious ranch-style house with a large basement and a manageable amount of yard, on a quiet street.

One of the things Daddy liked most about the house on Pine Tree Road was the fact that there was only one traffic light for him to be con-. cerned with in the 20-minute ride between his home and his office, some eight miles away. The hours that he commuted, however, posed little problem for heavy traffic. He rarely travelled during rush hours and was usually behind his desk long before dawn and home long after sunset.

One of the most memorable remarks about the house in McLean came from a constituent from Charleston who was on a visit to the nation's capital. Mother was told by the visitor's hostess that he had been more interested in seeing the home of Congressman Rivers than anything else. When he was driven past it, his only comment was: "*That's Mendel Rivers' house? Well, at least, he's honest!*"

Daddy was not known for being part of the social whirl of Washington. For one thing, he was always up early and liked to get to bed relatively early in the evenings. And, although he was never prudish about others drinking in front of him, he knew he was better off away from it.

When he showed up at a party, it was often reported in the newspapers of Washington, because it was so unusual.

When I was living with him before Mother moved up, I sometimes accompanied him to large functions where much was made over him. People rushed up to shake his hand, reporters and photographers wanted just one minute of his time. Luci Johnson, the President's daughter, gave him a big hug and called him "Uncle Mendel," much to my surprise, at a Democratic reception.

But we always left at the earliest possible polite opportunity, much to my regret. He needed to get to bed so that he could tackle things before dawn the next morning.

When Mother arrived in Washington, she was overwhelmed: "If I had thought it exciting to come to Washington as the wife of a Congressman in 1940, which I did, it was nothing compared to how I felt as the wife of the Chairman of the House Armed Services Committee.

"Many times I felt like Cinderella at the ball. At times we had a stack of invitations a foot high to various functions. Almost overnight there was a sudden new interest in us. I expected people to hang on Mendel's words, but they became much more interested in my conversation, as well."

CHAPTER 11

Secretary of Defense Robert S. McNamara had gotten along well with Carl Vinson and no doubt expected the relationship to continue virtually unchanged with his successor. Vinson had earned the esteem of fellow Congressmen, Administration officials and members of the military throughout his long career, but it was generally conceded that he had not usually opposed what the executive branch proposed. In fact, some even hinted that the Pentagon got what it wanted but allowed Vinson to think it was his idea.

The spell was broken early. At a conference between the new Chairman and the Secretary of Defense, McNamara let it be known that Vinson had given him certain latitude. He seemed to be saying that he expected the same with the new committee head. After a few minutes, Daddy, growing weary of what he considered a patronizing attitude on the part of McNamara, leaned across the table and slowly drew out his words, "But, Mr. Secretary, you don't seem to understand; Carl Vinson's gone. He's gone. Article I, Section 8 of the Constitution of the United States of America says that *Congress*, not some *temporary appointee* of the President, is the one that raises armies and protects the public."

Daddy was quick to recognize McNamara's abilities. There was no question that he respected McNamara for his intellect. But they looked at things very differently. "He's the most capable individual I've ever run into," Daddy conceded more than once. But he seemed to feel that McNamara, a former "whiz kid" from the Ford Motor Company, paid too much attention to his computers, to his systems analysis methods and to the bottom line figures and far too little attention to the actual needs of the defense structure of the United States...particularly the actual needs of the men and women serving in uniform.

McNamara, had, after all, been the Secretary of Defense for four years prior to my father becoming chairman of his committee. His talents were well-known. He was, as David Halberstam described him in *The Best and the Brightest* "...a man of force, moving, pushing, getting things done...He pushed everyone, particularly himself, to new limits, long hours, working breakfasts, early bedtimes, moderate drinking, no cocktail parties. He was always rational...That McNamara had such a good reputation in Washington was not entirely incidental—he knew about the importance of public relations, and played that game with surprising skill....[His] mind was mathematical, analytical, bringing order and reason out of chaos. Always reason. And reason supported by facts, by statistics—he could prove his rationality with facts, intimidate others."

He, as much as my father, was convinced that the way he perceived things was the correct way.

McNamara may have had computers and statistics to back up his arguments, but Mendel Rivers had the U.S. Constitution. And Chairman Rivers immediately sought to strongly affirm Congress' role in running the U.S. military, as specifically prescribed by the Constitution. In referring to Article 1 of the Constitution, Daddy said many times—with emphasis: "I take this to mean that Congress has the exclusive right to deal with the military. I don't mean a quasi-right. I mean the exclusive right."

Within months after taking up the gavel, the House Armed Services Committee rejected legislation proposed by McNamara to merge the Army Reserve into the Army National Guard. Daddy then penned legislation to restrict the Pentagon from closing military bases without prior approval from the Congress, a measure advocated by McNamara.

President Johnson promptly vetoed the base closings bill.

Daddy had no choice but to offer an acceptable compromise: "We do not claim a victory in this dispute with the executive branch of government, but certainly we do not acknowledge a defeat...What we do claim is that certain principles have been established and that Congress is a partner with the executive branch in all matters involving our national security."

"Why, Secretary McNamara and I get along just fine," he told a reporter. "I just don't happen to agree with him on a good many things."

Daddy enjoyed, on many occasions, referring to the Secretary of Defense by placing emphasis on his middle name: "Robert *STRANGE* McNamara."

And the press seemed to delight in reporting the differences of opinion between the new Chairman and the Secretary. Daddy might well have delighted in them, too, but, in general, he tried to keep the proper perspective regarding their disagreements: "There are lobbyists for all manner of things on Capitol Hill, and labor has its unions, but all you've got is Mendel Rivers and his committee of 40 members...I try to follow in the footsteps of former Chairman Carl Vinson, making one resolve to work for our fighting men, regardless of snipers or any outside influences...I am glad to be with a panel which is with me. So many times it is opposite, as with some of my contacts with Mr. McNamara, which have been amplified, magnified and unjustly reported. The only difference is in our philosophy. I am more interested in the human than in a statistic."

Where the Pentagon sought more unmanned missile production, Daddy pushed for more manned military programs as being the best way of assuring a strong defense for this country. To channel exorbitant amounts of money into programs while slighting *manned* programs would, in his opinion, be an extremely grave error.

"I will still depend upon the ingenuity of the human brain in preference to the computer when a decision is to be reached," he said. "I haven't got anything against missiles, but I happen to know that amphibious forces [for example] need pin-pointed artillery support before and during their landings..."

Another major Rivers-McNamara battle was over nuclear-powered ships for the Navy. Daddy argued strongly for new surface ships to be built as nuclear propulsion vessels rather than be conventionally fueled, as were the new submarines being built. He greatly respected, admired and relied upon the expertise of Admiral Hyman Rickover, "the Father of the Nuclear Navy": "Nuclear propulsion has the fundamental advantage of permitting our warships to go anywhere in the world to deliver their combat payloads and to return, all without logistic support," Daddy said...."On the contrary, oil-fueled ships must be refueled every few days...We must plan for crisis. It is precisely in such situations that the super mobility, maneuverability and reliability of nuclear warships will give America an unequaled naval striking force...What counts most in war is military effectiveness, not cost effectiveness."

He accused McNamara's analysts in the Pentagon of studying *to death* the question of nuclear power: "This issue of a nuclear Navy is one of my basic disagreements with Secretary Robert S. McNamara."

Daddy kept up his fight for nuclear-powered vessels, and it seemed appropriate that when the keel-laying ceremonies for a $224 million nuclear-powered frigate were held in 1970, Daddy figured prominently during those festivities. It was probably no surprise that the ship was named the *South Carolina*.

Admiral Rickover was asked to introduce my father at the luncheon following the ceremony. Daddy's ardent admiration for the Admiral was returned when Rickover rather effusively gushed, "He is one of the great men of our Congress. He is dedicated to peace, but aware of the awesome responsibility our nation bears in defense of our freedom. Where our national security is involved he is brave, resolute, and stubborn. His legislative acts are heroic...No man possesses in so high a degree the peculiar awareness of military realities...He is one of the most unintimidable men in the United States...He does his duty as if he were going to live forever..."

Admiral Rickover went on at such flowery lengths that when Daddy finally got up to speak, all he could say was, "There is nothing left for me to say except let's eat."

Daddy was dead within a few weeks after the *South Carolina* keel-laying ceremonies.

But within six months of his death, my sister and I were honored by being asked to be sponsors for the *U. S. S. L. Mendel Rivers*, a nuclear-powered submarine. Keel-laying ceremonies were held in June of 1973. This tremendous tribute to my father by the Navy was, I know, due almost exclusively to the efforts of Admiral Rickover. The submarine, whose motto is "Rivers Delivers," was commissioned in 1975 and had Charleston as its home port.

Her first commander, Captain Roderic L. Wolfe, told me years later that being the skipper of the *Rivers* represented more than just the command of a sub: "In the 1960s, being in the military was not a popular thing to do. In those surveys designed to determine in which rank the public holds various career choices, the military usually ranked somewhere below dog catcher or professional wrestler. The unrest on college campuses and the opposition to the Vietnam war resulted in the tragedy at Kent State and the burning of NROTC buildings on come campuses. Events like those caused some of us to wonder if giving our most productive years to our national defense was a wise thing to do. "I always knew that, as a graduate of Harvard College, I could earn more money as a civilian but I also felt that defending this great country of ours was a worthwhile way for me to serve my fellow man. I didn't think that we should be looked down on for making choices like that...

"It was in that context that we saw your father as a friend. His untiring effort to raise the military's standard of living gave us a sense that somebody cared and that our efforts were appreciated and worthwhile. Not only did he persist in his pursuit of military pay raises, but he also supported legislation to provide more military construction money for military housing, commissaries and exchanges, etc. which confirmed his sincere, genuine efforts to care for the men in uniform....I was always confident that while L. Mendel Rivers was in Congress, there was a voice that spoke for me..."

Shortly before the *Rivers* was to leave Charleston (due to the closure of the naval base) for the new homeport of Norfolk, her captain, Commander Bradford McDonald told me that he, too, has a special sense of pride for this ship: "Every *Rivers* sailor has heard how the 'gentleman from Charleston' continually labored to provide his country with the best military, the best navy and the best submarines in the world...I was only 15 years old and most of my men were not even born when he died. Now, as I near 40, his legacy lives on in a way that would certainly thrill him...His portrait is conspicuously mounted in our wardroom as a reminder that what we do to preserve our freedom today may affect our countrymen 25 years hence. And deep in our hearts we are all proud and honored to be part of the navy's 'silent service,' a service which Lucius Mendel Rivers helped create.

Proposals by the Administration to offer re-enlistment bonuses to solve the poor retention statistics in the military only gave Daddy more fuel when calling for pay increases for the military.

One frustrated Navy wife wrote to him when she learned that her husband, an electronics technician, had decided to get out of the Navy: "...In the four years that he has been in the Navy, he has spent only one year on a boat. The rest of his time has been spent going to school at the Navy's expense. The government has a large investment in him...[His] nuclear and electronics training are becoming more valuable to private industry. This is what is luring him out of the Navy...In recent weeks, I have learned that all of the men I know on [his ship] feel exactly as my husband. In fact, as far as I was able to check, no one on the crew has re-enlisted since the boat was commissioned. There is something *wrong* here! If these men were paid more on a level with their civilian counter-parts perhaps more of them would re-enlist. Isn't it more economical to keep the experienced men aboard than to train new men who will in turn also get out of the Navy?"

Calls for any reductions in defense spending always got a strong reaction from Daddy. "Only a dreamer would eliminate any segment of our defense structure during this period of our lives...only a fool would disarm during our lifetime."

The House Committee on Armed Services disagreed with so many things that Secretary McNamara did that the committee called for four parallel investigations of McNamara's policies, declaring that no new Pentagon requests would be considered until the investigations were completed. "Nothing personal," Daddy told a reporter.

Time magazine said of the feud between Daddy and his committee and the Secretary of Defense: "...McNamara has had his jousts with con-gressional committees before. But never have so many lances been point-ed at him at once, and never by such aroused antagonists...The case against McNamara is easy enough to make on purely emotional grounds.

He has angered many senior military officers and legislators in a variety of ways. He strikes his critics as arrogant. He has brought proud service chiefs to heel, smashed old customs and prerogatives, scrapped weapons projects that had many champions, reduced Congress' influence in military affairs and eliminated or cut back 852 military installations.

"...McNamara's critics feel that they have picked up fresh ammunition against him. McNamara attempted, for instance, to reduce by half the $1 billion military-pay increase voted by Congress. From the greenest recruit to the most bemedaled general, from the swampy boondocks of Vietnam to the carpeted offices of the Pentagon, this stand brought the complaint among servicemen that their boss was not behind them...Most serious of all—considering McNamara's reputation as an administrator and planner—is the giant logistics bottleneck in Vietnam that is backing up ships and their precious miliary cargoes as far as Japan and slowing the U.S. war effort. If McNamara knows anything, say his critics, he should know about logistics."

Once when Daddy was on his annual district trip, his Charleston office received a call from Secretary McNamara who said he wanted to set up a meeting with the Chairman regarding the upcoming defense budget.

He told Daddy's aide, Mendel Davis: "I would appreciate your getting in touch with the Chairman and having him call me as soon as possible."

When Daddy received the message in Hampton County, he responded that he would call the Secretary when he got back to Charleston the next day. Mendel Davis said that the Secretary was waiting to hear from him *that* day.

"You tell the Secretary that Congress is in recess and I'm down here with *my* people and I'll call him back tomorrow," Daddy instructed.

"But, Mr. Rivers, I can't tell the Secretary of Defense that," Mendel protested.

"Just who do you work for?"

"You, Mr. Rivers."

"Then, you tell him that."

When Davis relayed the message, the Secretary said to tell the

Chairman that he'd be happy to meet with him in Washington the next week. When Daddy got *that* communication, he told his young aide to tell the Secretary that he would see him in Charleston, not Washington.

The Washington Post headlined a story on the meeting "Mohammed Went to the Mountain."

Secretary McNamara and Cyrus Vance, the Deputy Secretary, arrived the next week at the Charleston Air Force Base. Daddy insisted on driving them to his home to have their meeting rather than to meet at a location on the base.

A local radio station, for some unknown reason, called the base commander's office during the afternoon to say that the Congressman and the Secretary had been in an automobile accident—a totally unfounded rumor, fortunately, that was quickly squelched by the Air Force Base commander who had had a base car follow Daddy's car just in case anything *should* happen.

After meeting for a couple of hours in the living room, Daddy casually walked his two visitors around the yard, pointing out different varieties of camellias. When they reached the front of the house, television reporters and cameras were waiting to interview them for the evening news broadcasts.

Our black yard man Thaddeus was standing to one side watching the activities and was obviously delighted with all the excitement. Daddy called him to come over, saying, "Thaddeus, I want you to say hello to the Secretary of Defense who has come down here from Washington."

Thaddeus, with his impaired hearing, caught only a few words of the introduction.

"Oh, yes, Suh," he beamed as he bowed over McNamara's hand. "I *see*—you he secretary. I works fuh my boss here in Chas'ton and *you* works fuh my boss in Washington. Glad to meet yuh, Suh."

McNamara left the Defense Department post in 1968.

Daddy never let up in hammering away for a strong defense position. He argued for it with Democrats and Republicans—with Presidents, Secretaries of Defense and, especially, with the Congress.

Clark Clifford became the Secretary of Defense for the remainder of Johnson's Administration. Secretary Clifford said that the relationship that he had with Daddy was pleasant and "routine except for the fact that once or twice a month I would go up to his office and we would have breakfast together. On those occasions I would have grits. This was an unusual experience for me because those are the only times in my life I ever had grits..."

In a speech before the House late in 1970, Mendel Rivers appealed to his colleagues: "Decisions on the defense budget should be based on the simple question of national survival—and nothing more...The issue should be 'what is required to survive?; and not 'how should we allocate the national budget between defense and domestic programs?'...The final measure of our ability to survive as a nation in a hostile world will not be how well we have managed our domestic resources and domestic programs, but whether or not we have avoided and frustrated the forces of evil which would draw us into the crucible of war...If we fail in that endeavor, we will have failed in everything...The issue...is very simply how much money must we spend to insure out survival—since if we fail to demonstrate to the Soviet Union our determination to survive—the amount of money we spend for domestic programs will become merely an academic exercise."

The Russian press said after this speech that the United States should be "cleansed" of the likes of Mendel Rivers.

Earlier in the year an article in a Russian literary magazine likened him to a tyrannical war-monger, eager to fight no matter the cost: "It is doubtful whether there is any other legislator in the Capitol who is so crazy about the military-industrial complex...His speech, his world view, and his politics are soaked in gunpowder...From the heights of Capitol Hill Rivers watches vigilantly to see that the shadow of peace and relaxation does not fall on America...This is a very dangerous man...There is death in his red bag. At the touch of his finger the land of America will turn not only into gold, but also into a magnet attracting retribution."

My father's views on Communism were strong. But he was particularly vocal and outraged about the establishment of a Communist regime in Cuba...especially since the American government and press had so effectively aided its creation, an opinion shared by my father and many others.

He had first denounced Castro in 1959 when the American Society of Newspaper Editors announced plans to bring Castro to the United States for a series of appearances. Spearheaded by Herbert T. Matthews in front-page editorials in the *New York Times*, Castro was portrayed as a crusader who arose to free the downtrodden masses of Cuba from the evil regime of Fulgencio Batista. Castro visited this country as a hero, and, as Daddy put it during a speech on the Floor of Congress, "paraded up and down Pennsylvania Avenue, and spoke at the Press Club like a stuck jackass," then went on to New York where "he and his band of brigands finished by tearing up that hotel" (a reference to the excessive property damage the Cuban entourage had done in a Manhattan hotel). Support of Castro as a savior of the Cuban people was, according to Daddy, being done "at a staggering price to the security of the American people."

The American Ambassador to Cuba during those troubled years was Earl T. Smith, who later said that U.S. government agencies and the U.S. press played the major roles in bringing Castro to power. While conceding that Batista's government was corrupt, Mr. Smith said that "many influential sources in the United States are dedicated to the overthrow of all dictatorships. We helped to overthrow the Batista dictatorship, which was pro-American, only to install the Castro dictatorship, which was pro-Russian."

Daddy appealed for strong action against Castro who flaunted to the world his systematic blackmail, humiliation and ultimate take-over of all American interests in Cuba, which were sizeable. When speaking to the U.N. General Assembly, Castro publicly insulted future President Kennedy, calling him an "illiterate and ignorant millionaire."

In June of 1960, when many still doubted that Castro was a Soviet tool, Daddy told Congress: "90 miles from the United States, the most deadly form of government is daily, methodically, and successfully being set up. Its principal aim is the infiltration and takeover of all the countries of Latin America. Time is running against us—tomorrow is too late—for this country to act affirmatively...Unless we act now, we may be placed in a position of inferiority when the effect of Soviet scheming brings the problem to a head. And that problem—I again warn the Congress—is no longer just a Cuban problem. It is a real, defined, definite U.S. problem—

a hemispheric problem...Not only for the sake of the Cuban people, not only for the sake of our security, but also because our very survival is threatened by this little pipsqueak..."

There were 100,000 requests for copies of that speech, but it did not cause a ripple in the course of our government's policy towards Cuba.

Daddy pounded away, calling for an invasion of Cuba in December of 1961. "Every military man with nerve and sense enough to think now believes that invasion is necessary," he said.

In response to that statement, Daddy received a telegram from 150 Marines at Camp Lejeune, North Carolina: "We will be happy to follow you into Cuba, repeat, *follow* you..."

Daddy was able to laugh at himself when he received that message and turned the telegram over to newsmen!

By September, 1962, there was no question that Castro was being supported by the Soviets when the news broke that Russia planned to build a port for "fishing vessels" in Cuba. Then, and only then, did both Houses of Congress get alarmed enough to vote on a joint resolution calling for the prevention of Communist aggression in the Western Hemisphere "by whatever means."

"Whatever means" for Daddy was an immediate blockade of Cuba. He urged the action, saying, "If blockading Cuba brings war, let our boys die for America. They are not interested in Laos, they are not interested in Indonesia, they are not interested in Berlin. But they are damned well interested in America."

The House passed the joint resolution by a vote of 384 to 7.

But Cuba was not blockaded.

In 1966, Daddy warned: "There are those who once again put their heads in the sand and say, `We can trust the Russians. Let us reduce defense spending'...At this very moment there are seven Russian ships in the Gulf of Mexico, one guided missile light cruiser, one guided missile frigate, two submarines, one submarine tender and two tankers...It is not an act of kindness."

When a Cuban MIG, flown by a defector, landed safely at a base in Florida, without being detected until seconds before it touched down, Daddy ordered an investigation into the lack of surveillance by the Air

Force. He was incensed when he learned that the Department of Defense, as an economic measure, had suspended the patrolling of the straits between the United States and Cuba.

He never let up on Castro and the Soviets. In one of his last major addresses to Congress, delivered on his 65th birthday in 1970, Daddy warned that "we are on the brink of disaster," and urged the Congress to provide more money for self-defense.

The "abysmal absence of strength" on the part of the American government to deal effectively with the communization of Cuba was, in Daddy's view, one of the greatest tragedies in the history of this country.

My father once said that if Theodore Roosevelt could see what had happened to the Monroe Doctrine, "he'd turn over in his grave so fast that he'd look like perpetual motion."

CHAPTER 12

"The moment Eisenhower walks into Indochina, Eisenhower and Rivers part company," my father said in 1954. While not exactly a prophet, Mendel Rivers, and many others, predicted a tremendous slaughter if Americans tried to match manpower in Southeast Asia. The mind-boggling scope of the destruction in the war of French Indochina provided a powerful lesson for what might take place if Americans were to become involved.

After the defeat of the French, America's low-key role of providing "advice" gradually and steadily progressed far beyond that. It was in 1965, during my father's first year as Chairman of the Armed Services Committee, that the first American ground troops were committed to a fighting war. That changed everything. Even if Congress had not declared war, then, essentially, the Commander-in-Chief had.

Daddy was the first to admit that there were no simple solutions to resolving the conflict in a country as politically and socially unstable as South Vietnam. But he saw our commitment there, once made, as part of an overall effort to halting Communist aggression.

As always, Daddy was extremely vocal in expressing his opinions about what was happening in that tiny country on the other side of the world: "Military operations in that Southeast Asia nation require decisions—made by trained military professionals, not armchair strategists in a warm and comfortable foxhole in Washington, D.C."

This was a whole new ballgame in fighting a war, as Daddy and many others were quick to realize. While the politicians were arguing about the conduct of the war, so were the master creators of public opinion—the members of the media. And, for the first time in our history of sending our men into battle, all the horrible, explicit details of this unpopular conflict were spread across the pages of every newspaper, magazine and television set every day in living and bloody color.

Daddy came across sounding like a war-monger to some. When accused of being a "Hawk," he shot back at the critic: "Hell, who would you rather have fight your war, a Hawk or a Dove?"

Daddy first visited Vietnam in 1965, shortly after assuming his chairmanship. Ironically, on his way there, he had stopped briefly in South Korea to be honored by the government of this other Asian country which Americans had fought to preserve. (One of the members of Daddy's party on this trip was retired General Mark W. Clark, who had been the commander in chief in Korea in 1952.) While there, my father reviewed a military procession of young Korean soldiers on the way to duty in Vietnam, one of the scant few allies of the United States to offer assistance during the conflict.

After a brief stop in Tokyo, the Congressional party stopped on the Island of Taiwan, or Formosa, where they visited Generalissimo Chiang Kai-shek, President of Nationalist China, at his home in Taipei. When Daddy and General Clark were invited to join the Generalissimo for breakfast the next morning at 8:30, my father declined, saying, "Thank you, but I'm sorry. That's too late for me." They settled on a 7 o'clock breakfast meeting.

Daddy was a great admirer of Chiang Kai Shek. He ardently supported the cause of Nationalist China as being in the best interest of the United States. On at least one occasion, Daddy hosted a luncheon for Madame Chiang in the Capitol when she was in Washington. Mother kept up a correspondence with her and her nephew for many years, long after Daddy's death.

In Hong Kong, Daddy and other members of his group met with General William Westmoreland, who flew in from Saigon. The next morning, Daddy donned a flak jacket and returned with Westmoreland to the Vietnam war zone. Many years later, General Westmoreland told

Mother and me: "Mendel was very thoughtful when he requested that I come to Hong Kong to meet him; it gave me a break from Vietnam."

The visit made a deep impression.

Over the next couple of years, as U.S. forces got more and more bogged down in a ground war that was getting us nowhere, Daddy and a few others urged the maximum use of our air superiority. Certain "sanctuaries" had been created by politicians which could not be touched by U.S. flyers, and Daddy termed this policy "rubbing salt in the eyes of our dedicated military men." While carefully avoiding crucial military installations, oil supplies, missile sites and the like, well-trained pilots were being forced to aim for innocuous targets which did nothing to deter the might of the enemy. "Can you believe that we have dropped almost as many tons of bombs in Vietnam as we did on Europe in World War II and we still haven't been able to knock our North Vietnam's two-bit railroad system," he said.

He never let up in advocating victory, a position which, rather surprisingly, was not particularly popular: "We are now engaging in a war of attrition in Vietnam. It is the same kind of war that bled the French people. We can never hope to match the Chinese and the North Vietnamese man for man, and it is ridiculous to pursue this policy...Even though we are inflicting heavy losses on the enemy, we are doing so at a heavy cost to ourselves. Regardless of what it may be called, this is war and in war there is no substitute for victory."

If we were not in there to win, he said time and time again, then we should get out.

He praised General William Westmoreland: "...the good soldier that he is, has never publicly complained. He has functioned as a commander, with restraints and limitations that would have driven a lesser man to complete distraction...He does not even have any control over the selection of targets in North Vietnam...General Westmoreland needs no defense from me...But I notice an increasing tendency on the part of the press and the Monday morning quarterbacks to build him up for the fall guy. They predict his removal. I can assure you that any reassignment involving General Westmoreland will be to a position of even higher importance...The question is not whether we should remove

General Westmoreland—the question is whether we will ever start listening to General Westmoreland and start taking his advice."

Daddy strongly advocated the bombing of Hanoi and Haiphong, and openly announcing to the world in advance that U.S. planes were going to do just that.

Democratic Members of Congress (none members of the House Armed Services Committee, though) sent, on several occasions, letters to President Johnson voicing their opposition to Daddy's recommendations. Fearing greater Russian and Chinese involvement, his opponents said that "the likelihood of civilian casualties in North Vietnamese cities would undoubtedly produce a world-wide reaction against the U.S. Government."

"Let world opinion go fly a kite," Daddy responded to his critics.

He was much more concerned that the U.S. Government was rapidly becoming the laughing stock of the world; that the most powerful nation on earth was being brought to her knees by North Vietnam, a fifth-rate, insignificant country: "American prestige is at a new low. I do not have to point out that we are getting almost no help from our European allies in this crisis. The only contribution we have received from many of them—whom we saved in *two* World Wars—is criticism and gratuitous self-seeking, self-serving advice...I am sure your blood boiled as did mine when I saw the Communist parade in Le Havre, France, on television last night where the people of the city of Le Havre loaded a Russian ship with supplies for North Vietnam. This is the same port liberated by American troops 25 years ago. These are the same people whom the Communists slaughtered in Vietnam a short decade ago at Dienbienphu....I want the American people to never forget that the fountainhead of ingratitude lies in DeGaulle's France."

Further, DeGaulle effectively pulled France out of NATO and for a time left the Organization's security communications in jeopardy, again as a direct affront to the United States.

Furious, my father quite seriously suggested that the United States bring all the bodies of Americans who had died saving France back to this country to be re-buried here. A former staff member in the American Embassy in Paris told Frank Jameson that Daddy's proposal was "a bril-

liant political move." DeGaulle reportedly heard about Daddy's rec-
ommendation and recognized the adverse repercussions such an action
would have on Franco-American relations; he subsequently toned down
some of his tough talk regarding the United States. The proposal was
ultimately abandoned.

Daddy became increasingly frustrated, as did many others in the
United States, about the conduct of the war and he constantly called
for doing whatever was necessary to achieve victory—not win a popularity poll—and, especially, to end the conflict: "This thing is ridiculous. It's cowardly. We are more afraid of world opinion than we are
of victory...When I see these boys of ours coming home in this endless stream of caskets, of broken bones, broken bodies and broken hopes,
then I say to hell with this...I don't give a damn about world opinion...To hell with what any other country thinks. Those are *American*
boys spilling *American* blood in Vietnam and it's the opinion of the
American people that concerns me...What is so God-damned sacred
about Hanoi?"

He was given newspaper headlines two inches high when he demanded: "FLATTEN HANOI."

When he called for General Earle G. Wheeler, Chairman of the
Joint Chiefs of Staff, to come before his committee to brief its mem-
bers on a master plan to win in Vietnam, General Wheeler declined.
Daddy immediately issued a statement to the press demanding the
American people's right to know if there was no intention of winning
in Vietnam.

He was highly skeptical about the success of "peace talks" declaring: "The communist understands but one language, the language of
power and military might. When a communist sees his factories in ruin,
his bridges and railroads destroyed, his roads obliterated, in fact all of
his modes of transportation eliminated, then and only then will he
understand we mean business."

This war, so under-fought, so under-finished, tore the country apart
and is blamed for many more ills than, perhaps, it should be. By 1968,
it was obvious that the Administration's policies and public statements
had alienated it from the country. Both President Johnson and Secretary

of Defense McNamara, each in their own way, had failed. McNamara was virtually fired as Secretry of Defense and was appointed to head up the World Bank. Johnson, of course, no longer had control of his own Democratic Party and simply could not expect to win; he declined to seek re-election.

My father's concern for the fate of the Democratic Party in 1968 was expressed in a letter to me that fall: "I think the Democrats will catch Hell this year. Johnson's leadership has just about wrecked the Party. Somebody will have to revive it in '72—if at all."

In a way, it was rather sad. David Halberstam, in his book, *The Best and the Brightest*, put it succinctly when he said: "For McNamara, the great dream had been of controlling the Pentagon and the arms race, but the war had ruined all that. War Secretaries do not limit the power of the military, and to a large degree he had lost control. The war absorbed so much of his time, his energy, his credibility, that he had little to give to the kind of controls he might have wanted. It was not by accident that his name would come more to symbolize the idea of technological warfare than it would civilian control of military.

"Lyndon Johnson had lost it all, and so had the rest of them; they had for all their brilliance and hubris and sense of themselves, been unwilling to look to and learn from the past...He had always dreamed of being the greatest domestic President in this century, and he had become, without being able to stop it, a war President, and not a very good one at that."

Daddy once told Mother: "It sickens me to see how many people in positions of authority *do not care* how many boys are dying in Vietnam." To him, American boys were being used a pawns in a no-win situation. And, while young men were dying, being maimed for life and being taken prison in unknown conditions, full media coverage gave legitimacy to those who opposed their government's involvement in Vietnam·and called for disarmament. The morale of the men in Vietnam was understandably a major concern to Daddy.

The Charleston Army Depot was one of the places from which young soldiers departed for Vietnam. On at least one occasion, Daddy saw one of the troop ships off when it departed for Southeast Asia. As the newspaper reported it, one of the soldiers was overheard to say to one of his friends: "See that guy with the long white hair...he's the Chairman of the House Armed Services Committee. He's the one who got us the pay raise."

Daddy moved among the men, asking them where their homes were and chatting with them. To one he said: "Remember, and tell your buddies to remember, that while you're over there, we're going to take good care of you."

He worked to obtain free mailing privileges for those in Vietnam. When the first frankings appeared on letters in 1966, they bore the words: "Free, thanks to Rep. L. Mendel Rivers."

Daddy was especially touched by some of the attentions he received in return from the men in Vietnam. The main road of an Army company area in a remote area of the battle zone was named Mendel Rivers Parkway. He was notified in 1966 that 50 non-commissioned officers in Di An had spontaneously voted him the "individual most helpful to the Army." In response, he wrote: "Tell your men in Viet Nam that I am not going to let them down. I have just begun to fight for the dignity and respectability of the American fighting men." He was once given a Viet Cong carbine which had been captured by a Navy patrol in the Mekong Delta. Daddy had it mounted on a plaque and displayed prominently and proudly in his office.

Daddy's friend Frank Jameson recalled a time that he was with him when he spoke to a POW wives group in California. Daddy was asked what he would do if he had his choice of action in Vietnam. "Well, ladies," Daddy said, "I think I would give Hanoi an ultimatum that if they didn't stop some of the things they are doing right now, that we would bomb Hanoi with a hydrogen bomb."

Frank said that he was absolutely horrified that Daddy would tell that group that he would think of dropping a hydrogen bomb right where their husbands were imprisoned! But several of the ladies stood up and said, "Mr. Rivers, that's exactly what my husband would want."

It was a turbulent time in America in those waning years of the 1960s, and the war in Vietnam only seemed to make matters worse amid the race riots, campus protests and political assassinations. In some handwritten notes that Daddy made, perhaps in preparation for a speech, he expressed the anguish that he felt as he witnessed what was happening in the America around him: "This nation is divided—as never before—Vietnam—(a tragic blunder)...Racial strife...Campus unrest...Affluent society...Adult delinquency...etc. etc....No motivation...We are worse off now than before WWII...We are temperamentally and intellectually unprepared ...Yet the East is on fire and our arsenal is not modern—We are not clearly superior in any area. Yet our leaders continue to cut our military back and fail to give us the facts on our potential enemy...They fear China...They fear Russia...They fear Fulbright... And they fear fear itself...250 ships laid up—and we a maritime nation—No urgency on a new bomber to counter the Soviets— And with an aging missile force with only the Poseidon & the ABM to sustain us—Carriers—The drafting of young men—a horrible thing— The immoral thing is for a war that has no ending—Beatniks, Bums and addicts infest the large cities."

Daddy had absolutely no patience with those who would take the law into their own hands to correct what they conceived as wrongs in American society and American policy. For those who would defiantly burn draft cards or, worse, their country's flag, to express disapproval of the war in Vietnam, he called for prosecution to the full extent of the law, including fines and imprisonment. He introduced legislation calling for a maximum fine of $10,000 or a prison term of five years, or both, for desecraters of the American flag, which he said was "the only thing which signifies the only nation on earth capable of defending the freedoms to which all nations aspire." Most tragic of all, said Daddy, the war in Vietnam was prolonged and more deaths were caused because of the "contemptuous, deplorable and sickening protests of misguided people."

His office was besieged with mail from soldiers, military families and other frustrated Americans seeking answers to the anti-war demonstrations. The demonstrations, Daddy once pointed out, were being conducted by "beatniks and other kooks who oppose the war in Vietnam simply because they are yellow and scared to fight for their country."

Somehow, anti-war demonstrations seemed to cease when mandatory military service was ended.

Daddy was, along with all Americans, proud when young Cassius Clay returned bearing a Gold Medal from the Olympic Games in Rome. But he was thoroughly infuriated when the boxing champion refused to be inducted into the Army in the late 1960s.

He was a boxing enthusiast—indeed, he had great admiration for all athletes who worked to develop their natural talents to become tops in their fields. He enjoyed strong friendships with both Jack Dempsey and Gene Tunney (whom he had first met in 1935 at a Young Democrats convention in Milwaukee).

In his book *The Greatest*, published in 1975, Muhammed Ali (the name Clay took after becoming a Muslim) referred to Daddy as one of the main people in America to put forth a determined effort to force him into the Army. That failing, my father then allegedly worked to prevent Ali's ever fighting again in the ring. Ali did not pass the mental aptitude portion of a draft induction examination and my father did, in fact, speak out publicly. Saying that Cassius Clay's Army deferment insulted every soldier serving in Vietnam, he added, "Here he is, smart enough to finish high school, write his kind of poetry, promote himself all over the world, make a million a year, drive around in red Cadillacs—and they say he's too dumb to tote a gun? Who's dumb enough to believe that?"

Ali said in his autobiography that when he had come to Charleston to stage a charity boxing exhibition that Mendel Rivers had interceded at the last minute to prevent the fight. Even though contracts had been signed and approved by the Charleston City Council, my father had persuaded the Council to revoke the agreement. Ali seemed to imply that the objections were as much racially-inspired as they were to do with with his draft status.

A Charleston newspaper sought to clarify the local point of view after the incident, which some tried to portray as racially motivated. In an editorial headlined "Clay Convicted Evader of Military Duty," it said that Cassius Clay "has been denied facilities and otherwise discouraged from visiting any number of communities. Charleston is not unique in its objections. Many reluctant communities are outside the South. The objections were raised not on racial grounds but because Clay has refused to comply with laws of his country which millions of others have accepted without claim of discrimination. Not even Canadians wanted Clay when an appearance was under discussion..."

Sadly, Daddy occasionally heard from parents who sought his assistance in changing the orders that were taking their sons to fight in Vietnam. He told Mother that once a prominent newspaper editor came to see him in his office and wept openly because his son had been notified that he was to go to Vietnam. On another occasion, a fellow Congressman brought a suitcase to Daddy's office telling him that it was from a constituent of his whose son had just received his orders. When Daddy opened the case, he found it filled with cash. He returned it to the Congressman who had brought it to him.

Daddy was sometimes the recipient of "hate mail," usually anonymous, and the object of organized protests. Fortunately, demonstrations against him were never violent. He was the main speaker at the Navy Day banquet in Long Beach, California, in 1967, where a small, but vocal, group of anti-war protesters picketed. Mother, Peg and I were with him, and we were naturally alarmed, along with the policemen, to see such a demonstration—something our family had never before witnessed. Daddy simply ignored them. There was no confrontation.

A couple of years later, in San Antonio to address the state convention of the Air Force Association, Daddy walked up behind a small group of demonstrators, watched them for a few minutes, then remarked to his host: "There's no harm to them. Let them go ahead."

Daddy once spoke to a student assembly at the Webb School, where Frank Jameson's son was a student. Gard Jameson approached his father before the assembly and told him that the school's seniors were gunning for Mr. Rivers and would tear him to ribbons if allowed to question him. Frank assured him that Daddy could take care of himself, but that Gard could tell the students "to shoot their best shot."

After Daddy's short address, one of the seniors stood up and asked,

"Mr. Rivers, what would you think if your son had to go to war and what if he got killed?" Calmly, my father replied, "Well, son, I'd hate it. But I'd hate it just as much if you went and if you got killed. Somebody has to do this job."

While Daddy was often the target of verbal criticism and hostility, both he and Mother feared the possibility of a physical attack on him. Once, when leaving Griffith Stadium in Washington, a rock had been tossed at the windshield of his car, which carried the rather conspicuous license plate SOUTH CAROLINA-U.S. HOUSE OF REPRESENTATIVES-I (designating the First Congressional District). I think it was shortly after he became Chairman that he purchased a small handgun which he had registered through the District of Columbia Police Department. Daddy routinely drove to his office before sunrise and, besides a handful of Capitol policemen patrolling, was alone for hours before other Congressmen and staff members arrived. He often returned home after dark and sometimes to an empty house.

In 1970, he was in Los Angeles to speak and, as usual, had the pistol in his briefcase. He invited me to join him, as I was living in the area, and we stayed overnight in the hotel where the banquet was being held. When we returned to our rooms late in the evening, Daddy discovered that his briefcase was missing. That night he slept in my room rather than his own, and he seemed to sleep soundly, although I did not at all. I was later interviewed by FBI agents investigating the theft. I remember that the agents did not really seem to believe that there had even been a briefcase, much less a gun. The incident was never solved. Many years later, long after Daddy's death, Mother received a letter from the Los Angeles Police Department informing her that a gun belonging to her through her late husband had been recovered as part of a criminal investigation and asking her if she wanted it sent to her. She had no idea at the time what they were talking about and assumed it to be a mistake.

A major part of the anti-war movement revolved around opposition to and condemnation of the so-called "military-industrial complex." Criticisms leveled at the defense contractors were fueled in large part by the almost unbelievable sums being awarded to them. Because of

Daddy's position as Chairman of the Armed Services Committee and the Committee's responsibility for awarding defense contracts, he frequently found himself in a position where he had to vehemently defend the industry that produced the military hardware.

Daddy insisted that, contrary to some of the loudest critics, the defense and aerospace industries were not the enemies of social and domestic progress: "Where in the name of God would we be without the industrial complex...The frustrations of Vietnam, the student unrest, the anxiety over inflation, the unsolved domestic problems have all contributed to feed the fires of criticism. But we must not let these frustrations of the moment hide essential truths. We must have a strong, truly combat-ready national defense force. In modern context, that includes a large industry capable of producing the sophisticated systems of national defense.

"The fact that there have been errors and shortcomings and mistakes does not obviate the need for a military force and a great industrial base to support it...The alternative to our great defense industry would be government ownership of industrial plants. Many years ago that's how weapons were produced—and the system failed. To try it again would mean nothing less than the end of the free enterprise system.

"When I mention the cost overruns in Medicare or building federal dams, or the construction of housing projects, they don't want to talk about that. These are understandable cost overruns, to these starry-eyed liberals...I haven't seen these people complaining about putting a man on the moon. That's an industrial complex, too."

He was especially responsive to accusations that money was to be made from continuing the war in Vietnam. "I'm supposed to be the granddaddy of the hawks and I think we should get it over with as fast as possible. The longer the war lasts in Vietnam, the more somebody's going to make out of it. I don't believe anyone should make money out of people dying."

Daddy had ample opportunities to benefit handsomely from his position. There were probably countless occasions throughout his 30 years in Congress when he could have taken advantage of his elected office and the information available to him to make vast sums, as have, unfortunately, many who have held public office. The laws were extremely liberal regarding gifts and contributions during his lifetime, but Daddy never wanted there to be any question about monies he received. For all the various criticisms, large and small, levelled at him throughout his career, a question of his honesty was not one of them.

Joe Riley told me that Daddy would not accept any checks unless they came from individuals for campaign contributions, and only personal checks. He always wrote the contributor a personal letter of thanks. From the records that Joe kept over the years, there were apparently many loyal supporters but, for the most part, the contributions were not large amounts.

Joe recalled a time when a representative of a maritime union came to him with "something" for Congressman Rivers, requesting that Joe pass it on to Daddy: "A fellow came to me with an envelope so thick that I couldn't hold it. I knew there was money in it. I called Mendel in Washington, and he told me in no uncertain terms what to tell them they could do with their money."

Much of the honoraria from speaking engagement he sent to the Episcopal Church in South Carolina, either to his own parish or to his childhood minister, The Reverend Harold Thomas. Some 50 years after meeting this young boy in Berkeley County, Mr. Thomas wrote to Daddy: "Through the years I have followed with great interest your career and have been proud of the fact that I was your pastor when you were a boy on your father's farm near St. Stephen. I cherish fond memories of the hospitality extended to me in your old home and my association with your parents and sisters."

Daddy was once characterized in a magazine article as being "above money."

The local newspaper announced several months after my father's death that, when finally settled, the estate of Mendel Rivers amounted to $63,000.

CHAPTER 13

Like everyone in public life, Mendel Rivers had his critics and enemies. But the undisputed master of attack was Drew Pearson, author of the widely-read, syndicated newspaper column "Washington Merry-Go-Round."

When Daddy and Mother first went to Washington in 1941, they were invited to attend the wedding reception of Pearson's daughter, who married the son of an old Justice Department friend of my father. Many high-ranking and important political people were in attendance that evening, and stringent security measures had been established and were accepted by them as necessary, even for an occasion such as this. To gain admittance to the reception, held at the Carlton Hotel, the credentials and identities of all the guests were meticulously checked three different times.

Their first encounter with Drew Pearson was when they went down the receiving line to greet the wedding party. Mother remembers him as a handsome and sophisticated man. It was a happy occasion, of course, and Pearson was friendly and cordial to all the guests. My parents were favorably impressed.

They read Pearson's popular column and frequently listened to his Sunday evening radio broadcasts. As they learned more about the personalities in Washington, they gradually came to feel that his views were somewhat slanted and sensationalistic, but they had no reason to feel any animosity towards him.

Pearson had been around Washington for a long time and had become well-known for his frequent attacks upon powerful members of the political establishment. He had been honing his skill for years, writing a column since the 1930s that took on the prominent, from Presidents on down. Truman, the story has been told, called him a "son-of-a-bitch" on a nation-wide radio broadcast. House Speaker John McCormack's letter to him in 1965 was quoted by many: "It is not necessary for anyone to call you a liar because everyone, including yourself, knows that you are a liar."

He was powerful, in large part, because few ever openly challenged him. His gossipy column was syndicated, and there were few newspaper editors who would tamper with his material. By the mid-1960s, Drew Pearson was read in newspapers and heard over the radio by over twenty million people.

In the opinion of many, including some fellow newspaper reporters, Pearson, under the guise of exposing excesses in government, distorted facts. Former *New York Times* correspondents Frank Kluckhohn and Jay Franklin authored a book about Pearson in the mid-1960s that was far from sympathetic. In it, they quoted sworn testimony by Pearson before a Special Government Commission on Government Publicity and Publications, in which he unabashedly defended his right as a newspaperman to beg, borrow or steal any information and publish it if he saw fit. This included classified government materials, which Pearson would not reveal how he had obtained when specifically questioned.

"The newspaperman," Pearson testified, "within certain limits and with consultation and good conscience, has the right, under the law, to decide what should be published...There are all sorts of documents marked 'secret,' 'top secret,' 'classified' which may have only to do with some inefficiency in government, nothing whatsoever to do with security to the nation...When you have been operating in Washington a long time [as I have] and you have been operating through a war [World War II], when you learn the rules of censorship and try to live up to them, why, naturally, you have to make judgments of your own."

Unquestionably, Drew Pearson was aggressive and persistent when he determined he had something to "expose." He rarely knuckled under, true in part because few dared to challenge him for fear of either losing the battle or getting worse treatment from his pen. Some have blamed Pearson for the death in 1949 of James Forrestal, the first Secretary of Defense, because of vicious attacks which allegedly led to Forrestal's suicide. More recently, there is no denying that Pearson helped to cause the fall of Senator Thomas Dodd of Connecticut in the 1960s.

Kluckhohn and Franklin said in their book, Pearson "...is almost a government in his own right, conducting foreign policy and domestic affairs...Proclaiming that he serves the public by uncovering official hanky-panky, he has for years been a hatchet-man for special interests...Never in all human history has a single journalist commanded such influence, power and practical immunity from the laws which control ordinary reporters...His column never lacked readers even if it did not always command respect; it invited attention and did not worry itself over whether the interest of its readers was sincere or simply scandalized."

After Daddy had gained some influence in Congress, he became the subject of some of Pearson's attacks, which increased in brutality as long as Pearson lived. Pearson assailed Daddy for, among other things, being a Southern conservative, being Chairman of his committee by virtue of the seniority system, travelling too frequently, being fiercely anti-Communist and for having military installations in his district: "As Armed Services Chairman, Rivers has enormous influence over defense spending, which has increased in his backwater district in direct relation to his rise on the Armed Services Committee...It seems incredible that one man could have such power. Nevertheless, thanks to seniority and a largely-docile, military-minded committee, Rivers wields this power. As a result, he has been able to prevent any penetrating investigation of various military mistakes...Rivers has bull-dozed multi-billion-dollar decisions through his Committee..."

But the hardest-hitting and most consistent allegation was that Daddy was a national security risk because of his drinking. Pearson dug in.

There is no question that Daddy had a drinking problem. He knew it and he openly admitted it. It was, no doubt, a constant battle for him.

Once from California in the late 1950s, he wrote to my mother about a dinner party he had attended where a member of his Congressional group had had too much to drink: "...I took care of him and struggled home with him. I could see myself in retrospect—a good lesson. Alcohol is the worst thing on earth. I pray daily—'But for the grace of God, there go I...'"

Another time while on a trip to Europe, he wrote: "I enjoyed the day I spent in Paris—Easter Sunday there was out of this world—After early communion I want to flea market and then to Left Bank of Seine...Have not tasted alcohol so far—no desire or intention to. Feel like a million. Being chairman of this group, I am quite careful. I have *really* made a fine impression so far..."

In June of 1966, about a year and a half after Daddy had become chairman of the committee, one of Pearson's columns accused Daddy of being hospitalized due to drunkenness and thus delaying discussion of important military legislation in the House: "Five successive times the House Armed Services Committee was called to meet during the past weeks to approve a massive new military construction bill. But each time the Committee meeting was called off...The official reason was the absence of the Committee's silver-maned Chairman...reportedly hospitalized by bursitis. Real truth, however, is that Rivers has been drying out from a drunk. It was so serious that the chairman of the Armed Services Committee had to be taken to the Bethesda Naval Hospital."

When the House convened the day that the column appeared in the morning newspapers, the military appropriations bill, sponsored by Daddy, was up for consideration. Before deliberations began, though, his friend Speaker John McCormack offered a tribute to Daddy on his return from the hospital which was followed by more praise from other Members and ended with a standing ovation.

Daddy was genuinely touched by their show of friendship and support, which he realized was in response to what had been in the Pearson column, even though no one referred to it. "I'm not going back to the hospital," he quipped. "It's bad publicity."

Newsweek magazine reported that "Pearson himself is a Quaker who rarely drinks and never smokes. But Pearson's moral convictions may not be the only explanation for the attack on Rivers. A liberal since the days of the New Deal when he started his Merry-Go-Round, the columnist holds no affection for the conservative—and segregationist—congressman.

"Pearson's apparent personal distaste for Congressman Rivers was one factor that led *The Los Angeles Times* to spike the column. But many of Pearson's 500 U.S. subscribers ran it, though at least one paper sent the column to its lawyers before doing so. The lawyers may have to be called in again. Pearson says he plans more columns on Rivers, even though he's aware he has set off a new round of anti-Pearson criticism among newsmen and politicians."

Early the next year, Pearson ran numerous columns about my father being a national security risk. To make certain that the public got the picture, some of the columns appeared two and three days apart.

Late in February, the "Washington Merry-Go-Round" column stated: "One committee chairman to whom the standard [of Congressional punishment] must be applied is Rep. Mendel Rivers, D-S.C., who as chairman of House Armed Services Committee and as watchdog of the CIA listens to the nation's most sensitive secrets.

"Rivers, however, is a security risk. He can be trusted with a secret no longer than it takes him to gulp down a few jiggers of bourbon.

"Rivers' flowing white hair and thin, dissipated face might have come from the pages of a William Faulkner novel. He is a charming, likeable person. But he simply cannot hold his liquor. This is a personal tragedy, which might have remained a whisper in Charleston's fashionable drawing rooms except that he has made it a national problem...

"We have tracked down various witnesses regarding Rivers... Some are former aides who fear retaliation; others are military officers whose careers would be ruined if they were identified. So we will report he facts without identifying any but pro-Rivers sources.

"Most witnesses describe the Congressman as charming when he's sober, a terror when he's drunk. One military escort, who had to nursemaid him overseas, recalled the experience as 'horrendous...'

"The armed forces always took the precaution of assigning a military escort with a reputation for sobriety as nursemaid to Rivers on his overseas junkets. One escort insisted that the Congressman, who has been able to stay on the wagon for months at a time, behaved like a gentleman.

"Others had different recollections. In London, he was found romping through a hotel corridor in his undershorts. In Madrid, he tore the dress off a lady guide. Once he got a few drinks under his belt, he also had a disposition to order generals around like bellhops."

Several days later, Pearson wrote, "Investigating security risks is a favorite sport on Capitol Hill, where the spotlight is constantly seeking out supposed subversives who look as if they might be a threat to the nation. But while Congress has spent millions exposing Communists and non-conformsts, it has carefully protected its own security risks.

"Take the case of House Armed Services Chairman L. Mendel Rivers, D-S.C., who is briefed by the Joint Chiefs of Staff and the Central Intelligence Agency on their most secret operations. Yet alcoholism has made him the No. 1 security risk who, in any branch of government except Congress, would be barred from secret information.

"He is no less a security risk because he can't help his sickness. Witnesses have told us of finding the safe wide open and empty liquor bottles strewn around his office in the mornings. He has also returned from alcoholic escapades without the haziest memory of whom he may have shared confidences with."

Only a few days had passed before the "Washington Merry-Go-Round" column said, "What will the House do about Rep. Mendel Rivers, the powerful House Armed Services chairman whose drinking problem has made him a serious security risk? He has access to the most sensitive secrets of the Defense Department and Central Intelligence Agency; yet by any security standard, he can't be trusted with classified information.

"Rivers has also treated the Air Force as his private airline, commuting between his homes in Washington and Charleston and flying off on overseas junkets, often as the sole passenger in a huge Air Force jet."

It must have been one of his most welcome pieces of correspondence, in the midst of all this, to receive a short note from a retired Navy Commander in St. Petersburg, Florida, who wanted to make certain that Daddy knew that the *St. Petersburg Times* had not run a recent Pearson column. He enclosed a tiny announcement which appeared in the paper with the explanation: "Drew Pearson's Merry-To-Round column is omitted today because it contained repetitious material abut U.S. Rep. L. Mendel Rivers, D-S.C." The letter ended by adding, "My best wishes always and thanks for your support over the years. Faithfully yours..."

The next Pearson column, several days later, kept the fire going: "Rep. L. Mendel Rivers, the white-maned House Armed Services chairman, possesses such power over the Pentagon that the generals and admirals scramble to do his bidding.

"They have loaded his backwater district with so many military installations that it could wage a major war on its own. This has brought prosperity to the home folks...

"The Army leased three buildings in Rivers' district...The Navy has also expanded its Charleston Navy Base, which is now headquarters for the Polaris submarine fleet in the Atlantic...The Air Force also flies Rivers wherever he wants to go. The Navy provides him with ambulance service to the Bethesda Naval Hospital.

"The Joint Chiefs of Staff also give him top-notch briefings, though he has a drinking problem. Military officers have covered up Rivers's alcoholic problem.

"On at least three occasions, the Secretaries of the three services, Joint Chiefs of Staff and assorted other brass hats took time out from the Vietnam war to participate in home-town celebrations honoring Rivers.

"In October, 1965 [actually 1964], this glittering assemblage of high defense officials stood through a downpour in North Charleston while Mrs. Rivers unveiled a bronze bust of her husband gazing majestically down from a seven-foot granite shaft."

The columns were painful to all of us. Pearson twisted and embellished the facts with sometimes outrageous fabrications, but some of what he said was true, and other things could possibly have been.

These were still the days when the press, just as it had been a mere few years before with John Kennedy, considered a politician's private life just that. Politicians who drank, and many did, were accepted as the norm. Unless someone did something in public that could not possibly be ignored, it was left alone.

William "Fishbait" Miller, for 28 years the Democratic Doorkeeper for the House of Representatives, said in his book *Fishbait* that "...the public is lucky. Unless a congressman jumps into the drink after a pretty girl—'a la Mills' [Wilbur Mills]—or lands a punch on a fellow lawmaker in full sight of everyone—which has also happened—nobody knows except the intimates on the Hill and public illusions remain safe...The Hill crowd merely laughs about drinking problems. Mendel Rivers was fair game for the jokesters....[T]he big joke on the Hill was that if he, as chairman of the Armed Services Committee, got even one more military installation for his state, he would sink the shoreline and put Charleston completely under water."

The military, who could thank the Armed Services Committee chairman for a great deal did, in fact, try quite hard to please him. He did fly in Air Force planes between Charleston and Washington (although members of his family never did). And there was a lot of "brass" standing in the rain on the day that the bust of my father was unveiled in 1964.

I know that my father drank on some of his trips abroad. My mother witnessed a couple of them, much to her dismay. I have no doubt that military escort officers protected him.

The times that my father was drinking do not stand out in my mind from the years of my childhood. He was never abusive. He despised himself for the weakness. And he was very concerned about how the Pearson columns affected his family. They, of course, did affect us.

The most hurtful aspect of all the Drew Pearson stories was the suspicion that someone employed in Daddy's Washington office had worked with Pearson's staff to help create the stories. A man once came into Daddy's office to tell him that "leaks to Drew Pearson were coming from within." There was, in fact, enough truth in the Pearson stories that only an insider would know. Daddy, who quite naturally expected loyalty above all else from those he hired, handled the matter quickly and quietly; a member of his staff was let go shortly thereafter.

The columns continued. Daddy received letters from around the country both from people who believed the stories and from those who sympathized with him. Many who disagreed with his politics came to his support because of the vindictiveness of the attacks. Many others asked why, if the stories were lies, he did nothing about them. Some could not understand how he could continue to put himself in a position to be criticized.

One of Daddy's colleagues in the House, asked by a Washington reporter about the allegations regarding Daddy's drinking, dismissed the charge as "garbage," adding that he had seen Mendel Rivers "under the weather twice in nine years...I've been drunk more often than that."

Jack Anderson, Pearson's assistant, once visited Charleston hoping to get some hometown criticism of Daddy for a story. He had plenty of nerve, actually, when he paid a call on Joe Riley and asked to see the records of Daddy's campaign funds. Joe, a tall man, told Anderson, an even larger man, to get out of his office or he would physically remove him. Shortly thereafter, Anderson authored a scathing column about Joe and his control of "Rivers' cash register."

In private, Daddy referred to Pearson in extremely strong terms, but not often. Publicly, he said very little. He did tell one newspaper reporter: "I don't think my drinking is what Pearson is really getting after. I don't know what he is after. But I think this attack is aimed at the things I stand for and what I have been trying to do with this committee...I also think Pearson is attacking the Congress, for its daring to differ with the Pentagon and for its stand in support of me and my committee in upping our defense program above and beyond what [Secretary of Defense] McNamara wants.

"I am quite sure that this is an attack on the belief that Congress has the constitutional right to 'raise and support armies' to defend this country sufficiently."

Daddy refused to dignify Pearson by responding to his accusations.

While not exactly a national debate, the dilemma which my father faced in persuing legal action against Pearson was the subject of a Columbia University *Journalism Review* article which appeared in the spring of 1967. Author Donald R. Shanor pointed out that, recent rulings of the Supreme Court guaranteeing freedom of speech "broadened the right of the press to criticize public officials, even if some or all of the facts are wrong."

Interviewing my father by telephone, Shanor quoted him as saying "That doggone Supreme Court decision...didn't give Pearson the right to lie, but it did encourage his recklessness."

My father had, in fact, had attorneys study the possibility of a libel suit against Pearson. Such an action would have been quite risk-taking from Daddy's point of view.

One evening at a White House reception, Daddy spotted Pearson across the room. "There's Pearson. I'd like to kill him right now," he confided too loudly to Mother. She begged him to be quiet and was greatly relieved when he didn't accost his enemy. However, she recalled, "If looks could kill, Mendel could have polished Pearson off easily."

Pearson did not let up.

In a 1968 column he said, "...the Defense Department budget was passed in two hours by Rep. Mendel Rivers, the silver-maned solon from South Carolina who has sometimes been so addicted to alcohol that he has been unable to pilot arms legislation through Congress...The Congressman from Charleston, incidentally, has been trying to block a book, "The Case Against Congress," [written by Pearson and Anderson] to be published by Simon and Schuster next week, because it deals with some of his extracurricular activities.

"During the Defense Department debate this year, however, Rivers was cold sober. 'Drew Pearson has put me on the wagon,' he confided to colleagues."

Drew Pearson died in 1969, and with him, many of the most vicious attacks of the press upon Daddy. Kathy Worthington said that on the day that Pearson's death was announced, Daddy came into the office and exclaimed: "Well, if Drew Pearson gets in Heaven, *nobody* will have to worry about getting there."

CHAPTER 14

Mendel Rivers could, at the height of his political prominence, feel confident about his standing with his constituents back home. There was one election, however, that posed a threat to him.

In 1968, black attorney George Payton, Jr., opposed Daddy for the Democratic nomination in the primary. Interestingly, the young Charleston attorney's main criticism of Daddy was his strong support of the military both nationally and locally—the very things that were so much a part of Daddy's strength in his district.

Throughout the campaign, Payton accused Daddy of being a warmonger and called for an end to the war in Vietnam. He criticized him for his role in having a heavy defense-related economy in the First Congressional District, and called for a more diversified economic arrangement.

Even though many of the black leaders throughout the district opposed his entering the race against Daddy, Payton insisted that he would carry the black vote and ultimately win in the general election and better represent the district in Congress.

While not worried about Payton's campaign promises nor the attacks upon his record and accomplishments as Congressman, Daddy *was* concerned about the relatively new, but growing, strength of the Republican Party in South Carolina. Voters were allowed to vote in the primary of the political party of their choice. Republicans were understandably anxious to demonstrate their might in the political make-up of the state by supporting their own candidates in the Republican primary.

Thirty-six percent of the district's voters were black and, presumably, 100% Democratic. The real threat to Daddy's winning was low voter turnout of white conservatives, normally his ardent supporters, who would choose to vote in the Republican primary rather than in the Democratic.

For the first time since the campaign of 1940, Daddy had to campaign fairly actively for the Democratic nomination. This time he did not have to make pledges about what he would try to accomplish for his constituents, but, rather, could point to his record of the previous twenty-eight years.

But this was 1968 and this was the year that is remembered as one of the most disturbing and volatile years in America. Tension was high. Students rejected authority and turned campuses into battlegrounds. Race riots in the nation's largest cities ran out of control. Popular leaders like Martin Luther King, Jr., and Robert F. Kennedy were assassinated. The President of the United States, Democrat Lyndon Johnson, under the pressures of the Vietnamese conflict, announced that he would not seek re-election.

Republicans were out to win and to turn things around in America.

This was the first time that any member of the Rivers family had been called upon to participate in one of Daddy's campaigns since Mother had worked with him in his first campaign for Congress. It did not take any of us long to realize how completely sheltered we had been from many of the brutal realities of the political world. Few politicians are returned to office with such virtual ease as my father had been throughout his career.

At the time, I was living in San Francisco and was able to take a couple of weeks away from my job to return to Charleston and help in Daddy's campaign. When I arrived, I found to my dismay that no one seemed as concerned about the election as I was. A campaign organization was in place, but it lacked the spit-and-polish, high gloss of ones I had witnessed in California.

The most important thing to get across to the voters was not a blast of high-tech political advertising but an understanding of the election laws governing primaries. The second most important thing was to encourage both white and black voters to come out for Mendel Rivers in the Democratic primary. Billboards were erected, television spots were taped (the first, I believe, Daddy ever did), bumper stickers were printed and brochures were churned out. It was not slick, but it was saturating and effective.

"RIVERS DELIVERS" again became a popular campaign slogan. Campaign literature urged the voters to remember that Mendel Rivers "...is important to you here in the First Congressional District. He is important to America. It is YOUR responsibility to re-elect him. YOUR OPPORTUNITY TO VOTE FOR HIM IN THE GENERAL ELEC-TION DEPENDS ON YOUR VOTING FOR HIM IN THE DEMOCRATIC PRIMARY. He is especially important to you since you live in the First Congressional District. He's not only done things for America, he's done things for you! VOTE FOR RIVERS IN THE PRI-MARY."

Since Daddy had not had any viable opposition in many years, there was not an organized army of volunteers to call upon to do the endless jobs necessary to put materials into the hands of all of the registered voters throughout the district. But hundreds of people enthusiastically helped to get out the vote for him. It was a rather exhilirating time for all of us.

My brother, a student at Georgetown University, brought a carload of friends down from Washington to pitch in for the effort. They spent their days driving all over the district handing out brochures and bumper stickers. Mother says that about all she contributed during that campaign was constant meal preparation for all the people who were suddenly in residence—a vitally important task.

Daddy's constituents, both white and black, did not disappoint him. While his Republican constituents might not have agreed with his party, it was obvious by their turnout that they agreed with him. A Republican party poll watcher was seen voting in the Democratic primary booth.

He won by a four-to-one margin.

Dr. James B. Edwards, the Charleston County Republican chairman, ran in the Republican primary as a "ghost" candidate for the First

Congressional seat. He publicly expressed pleasure, though, at Daddy's victory in the Democratic primary and did not oppose him in the general election in November.

Daddy later told Mother that George Payton had come to him several months before the primary and had confessed that he did not really want to oppose him, but had been urged to do so by some blacks in the district. Daddy had nothing against Payton and had told him, "Oh, that's all right. Go ahead and oppose me if you want to."

Almost by default, Daddy emerged as *the* Democratic leader in South Carolina in 1968. At a time when Republican strength was rapidly increasing, the Democrats saw him as the only person powerful enough and popular enough to keep the eroding ranks somewhat together in the state. Old-line Democratic Party regulars could not go along with the national party nominees and openly supported the Nixon-Agnew ticket. Charleston's Mayor Palmer Gaillard, a loyal Democrat for many years, came out for Nixon.

Daddy, of course, owed his seniority in Congress to the Democratic Party, but he never gave up his prerogative to express what was often philosophically different from the party "line." He openly said that he supported many of the views of the third party candidate, former Alabama Governor George Wallace. (Governor Wallace once approached Daddy about running on the ticket with him.)

Mendel Rivers was politically conservative and South Carolinians knew it, even though he was considered the most liberal member of the South Carolina delegation. He had voted for the food stamp plan, the Peace Corps, the mass transit bill and the poverty program. Daddy was comfortable with his voting record. "I had an awfully hard time when I was a young fellow," he pointed out. "I knew poverty like nobody else in the South Carolina delegation ever did. Whenever I can help the man in the street, I'll do it."

He had plenty of critics on the other side of the political spectrum, as well. The Catholic Bishop of Charleston, The Most Reverend Ernest Unterkoefler, once sent him a wire urging him to "Vote for civil rights bill now on Floor of House—Open Housing included. Urgent that you demonstrate leadership for equality and non-discrimination in South

Carolina."

The next day Daddy responded with a telegram that read: "Thank you very much for your gracious wire relative to the civil rights bill and open housing. Concerning my demonstration of leadership I respectfully remind you that I took an oath to support the Constitution of the United States. I consider open housing legislation as now written a violation of every precept of ownership of property guaranteed by the Constitution. I consider it my duty to oppose the legislation to which you refer."

In September of 1968, placing Daddy clearly at the helm of a show of party unity, local Democrats gave him a birthday party at Charleston's municipal auditorium. Daddy, enjoying his role but refusing to take it too seriously, declared to the audience that no one had any reason to apologize for being a Democrat since, he added, "We Democrats do as we please." Charleston County Democrats appreciated the remarks of their Congressman, particularly since many felt uncomfortable with the national Democratic ticket of Humphrey and Muskie.

Remarking on the Democratic birthday celebration, the newspaper editorialized: "It is perhaps premature to call the local Democratic Party a Rivers party, but sometimes we see it trending in that direction, if only informally. The arrangement, though unusual, would have a certain appeal...A Rivers Party might have mule ears at one end and an elephant's trunk at the other but it could be a creature in joint with the times."

Local Republicans accused their Democratic opponents of riding into office on Rivers' coattails. Senator Strom Thurmond, a Republican since 1964, even announced to the press that it would be worth the loss of Daddy's position as Chairman of the Armed Services Committee to have Republican control of the Congress. But, he said, he implied no personal animosity and affirmed their long-time friendship. Thurmond might, when issuing that statement, have recalled Daddy once declaring "I could whip Thurmond any time I want to," when he had been urged to oppose him for the Senate seat.

After the general election, there were rumblings about a move among House Democrats to censure Daddy for appearing with Governor George Wallace and his running mate, Air Force General Curtis LeMay (a man for whom Daddy had great admiration), during the campaign. Nothing ever came of it.

The next spring, in 1969, Daddy and his position in Congress again came under fire in the district. This time it was not partisan politics, but a local labor dispute, fraught with racial controversy, and one which gained a great deal of national publicity.

In March, 12 nonprofessional black employees of the Medical College Hospital, the state teaching facility, demanding recognition of their union, walked off of their jobs and were subsequently fired. Picket lines in support of the workers' action appeared at the hospital. When picketers violated a court order limiting the number of protesters, many arrests were made. Hundreds honored the picket lines and stayed away from their jobs. After the failure of local black clergy to resolve the dispute, the Rev. Ralph D. Abernathy, head of the Southern Christian Leadership Union came to Charleston in a show of support for the hospital workers and the union.

Picket lines appeared at other hospitals in the area, protest marches and rallies were organized, and the dispute remained deadlocked for weeks. Coretta Scott King, Martin Luther King, Jr.'s widow, came into town to lead a protest march of 2,000 persons through the medical complex.

Abernathy accused just about everyone in a position of authority in the state of allowing conditions to exist in South Carolina which forced the hospital workers to strike for improvements. Of Mendel Rivers, he said that he was willing to spend sixty percent of the national budget "for the destruction of life on foreign battlefields, $25 billion to send a man to the moon, but is unwilling to spend billions of dollars to stand people on their feet in Charleston."

As the strike dragged on, with no end in sight, tempers got short and some acts of violence did occur, though none severe. But it was enough to convince Governor Robert McNair to call out the National Guard to help maintain order. Ultimately, a curfew was ordered for the city of Charleston and parts of the county. The last time that the SCLU had become actively involved in a union strike had been in Memphis the year before, when Martin Luther King had been killed.

My future husband, René Ravenel, then a medical student, said that he was on his way to the hospital early one morning, when he rounded a corner and a National Guardsman halted his car and stuck a rifle with a fitted bayonet into the window. The Guardsman turned out to be a friend he had known for years. He immediately apologized, saying: "They told me to do this!" He followed his orders. He asked René a series of questions, then feeling confident that René was telling the truth and did not intend to create a civil disturbance, allowed him to proceed to the hospital.

Daddy did not wish to have any involvement in the strike, and insisted that it was not a federal matter and that he should not make any statement about the situation. But when the Department of Health, Education and Welfare sent investigators to Charleston to look into charges of racial discrimination, Daddy fired off a letter to HEW Secretary Robert Finch: "Discrimination against whom? Is your department investigating discrimination against the sick in the hospitals—some of whom are at death's door—and whose treatment has been disrupted by this strike and its attendant pickets, marches and demonstrations?...Have you ordered an investigation of the discrimination against the merchants and citizens of this community whose lives and incomes are being devastated by the disorder accompanying this strike and by the measures that must be taken to preserve public safety? Is your department investigating the discrimination against those whose property has been damaged by brick-throwers, fire-bombers and looters?"

Our home was picketed on at least one occasion that we heard about. The protesters dispersed when they realized that no one was at home.

It took nearly three months for the dispute to be settled.

While the strike did not become the national issue that some thought it would, there was a good deal of publicity surrounding it in many parts of the country, no doubt because of the SCLU participation. Even *Pravda*, the newspaper of the Communist Party in the Soviet Union, wrote about the strike: "The strike lasted three months...During this time, many people were brutally beaten unmercifully...But the strikers did not give up...The just struggle of the hospital workers has aroused a wave of solidarity...In the plot against the workers...Rep. Mendel Rivers play[s] an active role."

The SCLU selected Charleston for its annual convention shortly after the strike settlement. The Rev. Andrew Young, who would later serve as the U.S. Ambassador to the United Nations under President Jimmy Carter and as Mayor of Atlanta, was a SCLU official and told a newspaper reporter that the convention site was selected partly in an effort to try to build up opposition to Mendel Rivers: "We're seeking to put him out of office as a symbol of the kind of racism and militarism which we think has kept the entire nation enslaved...He symbolizes all we have fought against...This is the district that elects Mendel Rivers to Congress and Mendel Rivers is almost the czar of militarism in America...Because so many of our racial and economic problems grow out of our over-expenditures in the military, that makes Charleston a fitting place for work for years to come."

Apparently, all blacks did not share the views of Abernathy and Young. An editorial appeared in a black newspaper which admonished many in the black community: "Every Negro citizen should resent Abernathy or any other outsider coming into our State telling us whom we should vote for or against. The Negroes of Charleston know Congressman Rivers better than any outsider...We certainly think more of, and have more respect for Congressman Rivers than we do Abernathy."

William Saunders, a black leader in Charleston later said of Daddy: "I personally look on Mendel Rivers as a racist. A lot of younger blacks share that view. But the black community itself has a lot of faith in Mendel. He's done a lot of things for Charleston, and I don't fight that. A man who was starving before can now go to Avco which manufactures gas turbines for helicopters and make $2.35 an hour just sweeping the floor."

After Daddy's death, Mother received a letter from General "Chappie" James, the highest-ranking black in the Air Force, who told her: "I have lost my best friend."

CHAPTER 15

On a Friday morning early in December of 1970, Mendel Rivers arrived at his office on Capitol Hill, as usual, before dawn. By the time his staff arrived around eight o'clock, he had already gone through foot-high stacks of correspondence and summaries of legislative bills requiring his attention. In the quiet of the early hours, he polished up the presentation he was about to make before the U.S. House of Representatives.

My father was completing his 30th year in the U.S. Congress and his sixth year as Chairman of the House Armed Services Committee. After the election the previous month, he had told my mother that he would not run for office again.

The resolution that he was to present that day for adoption by the House was one for which he felt especially strong passion. It had to do with American prisoners of war being held by North Vietnam.

Peace talks to formally end the hostilities in Vietnam had been going on for some time in Paris, but the issue of American prisoners had constantly bogged down the discussions, such as they were. North Vietnam had, with frustrating constancy, called American military involvement in the conflict a criminal action. It had refused to adhere to the terms of the Geneva Convention of 1949 which it had signed, claiming that those terms did not apply because U.S. participation in the fighting was illegal and that the captured Americans were not merely combatants, but, rather, outright criminals. Furthermore, it would not reveal the identities of the prisoners, refused to allow inspections by the International Red Cross, would not allow the exchange of mail between prisoners and their families, and steadfastly refused to release sick and injured prisoners—all violations of the Geneva Convention.

To make matters worse on the already-frayed emotions of Americans at home, it was known that, among other atrocities, North Vietnam held American prisoners in conditions below standards of human decency; allegedly, many prisoners were kept in bamboo cages designed for captured jungle animals.

Over the weekend of November 22nd, 1970, a daring attempt had been made to rescue American prisoners believed held at Son Tay, near Hanoi. The rescue forces successfully entered the prison compound, but found it empty and realized that the prisoners had probably been abruptly moved to another location. Naturally, Hanoi assailed the raid, promising to punish Americans for it. Even worse, anti-war opponents at home also condemned the action as ill-conceived and damaging to the peace negotiations.

When Mendel Rivers stood before his colleagues in the House, he urged them to support what became known as the "Tiger Cage Resolution," an official commendation for the members of the rescue effort for their heroism. And far more importantly, he prevailed upon the Congress to pointedly express its concern for American prisoners of war by insisting that negotiations in Paris cease until substantive progress had been made on the prisoner issue.

"We've been powerfully patient with this bunch of heathens...I want the world to know that I would tell that crowd in Hanoi, you will either treat them [the prisoners] with human dignity or some of you will not be here tomorrow...

"So far as I am concerned, if I were President of the United States, I would deliver an ultimatum to this crowd and let them guess where the next blow was coming from."

Opponents of the resolution argued that the commando raid, while heroic, had been a political disaster and that tying the prisoner question to the peace talks would result in no negotiations at all.

Daddy reminded the Congress that the Paris meetings had just passed their 93rd session with no progress at all!

The resolution was adopted by the Congress.

The next day, Saturday, December the fifth, 1970, a Pan American World Airways jet touched down in Oakland, California, with 198 military men, the majority of them enlisted, for a Christmas furlough from Vietnam.

Dubbed "Operation Reunion," this was the first in a series of flights that was due, in large part, to efforts by my father to obtain affordable fares and services for servicemen on duty in Vietnam. "Reunion" was a cooperative effort of the United Service Club and Pan Am which reduced the regular fare from $969 to $369, a price which vastly undercut the Pentagon's boast of obtaining a $700 ticket!

The first planeload of men brought with them gifts and praise for their friend, Mendel Rivers, for his role in the program which brought them home. Actor Jimmy Stewart met the plane and was asked to make certain that he got them.

A couple of days later my father was presented with a cap emblazoned with six stars reading "The Big Boss"—outranking any military officer. In addition, the soldiers sent him a long scroll praising him for his airfare plan signed by "your boys in Nam;" a brass gong bearing the message "When you ring people sit up and take notice;" as well as a wristwatch with the inscription "You watch over us."

My father proudly put on the hat and flashed a big smile for the photographers who took the last picture of him.

The day after, December 8, 1970, after handling routine matters in his office, my father departed for Birmingham to be admitted to the University of Alabama hospital for open heart surgery.

Never one to discuss his personal affairs, Daddy told virtually no one about the impending surgery except members of his family. Even then, heart surgery had become so acceptable and so routine that all of us took it in stride. There had never been any consideration that his children should be at the hospital when he had the surgery.

A short press release was issued from his office announcing that he had been admitted to the hospital. When Charleston newspaper reporter Barbara Williams talked to him by telephone at the hospital, he told her to tell any politician waiting to take his place that it was premature: "I'm not going to die yet."

The attention that Daddy's hospitalization stirred up was fairly over-whelming and extremely heartwarming. From admirals and generals to privates and airmen, constituents and total strangers, cards, letters, flow-ers and telegrams arrived in Birmingham.

I do not know which newspaper it was, but I learned later that an unsigned advertisement appeared in the classified section of a major paper which read: "Attention all service men. Our greatest friend, Rep. L. Mendel Rivers, is undergoing heart surgery at the U. of Alabama Hosp., 1919 7th Ave. S., Birmingham, Ala., 35233. Let's show apprecia-tion—send cards." They didn't let him down. Hundreds of letters and cards from around the world poured in from military personnel: "As an Air Force family, we consider you our best friend in Washington…"

"Saw in the paper you're in the hospital—Never written a man so important before so don't know how to put it—Get well—I've always admired you for years—was going to write you thanking you for all you've done for us but have put it off until now. Once again, thanks from all the service people. Get well soon. We need you."

"Although many people have undergone this operation, I doubt whether anyone has ever had so many enthusiastic supporters rooting for the individual concerned."

"I believe I speak for most GIs when I say you are in our minds and hearts during your hospitalization…Get well soon, and remember the thoughts and prayers of thousands of GIs are with you at this hour."

"I read in the morning paper of your scheduled surgery. My sincere hope is for your speedy recovery. In this day of spinelessness, there are too damn few people in the legislative branch of our government who possess your forcefulness."

"A gentleman that works his heart out for us deserves all the good things god can offer him. Wishing you all the best and future good health."

The first and only time I ever heard my father say anything about his heart condition was in the summer of 1969. He rather casually complained of a slight chest pain as we were walking up a small hill in the German town of Berchtesgaden where we had gone for a rare family vacation.

For several years, though, many physicians had urged my father to have an operation to repair the mitral valve of his heart. He had put off the surgery but had consulted a number of doctors, hoping, of course, to find one who would disagree with the diagnosis of the others. Finally, after visiting the Heart Clinic in Miami, he accepted the fact that the surgery was inevitable. On the unanimous approval of all of his physicians, the chief of surgery at the University of Alabama, Dr. John Kirklin, scheduled his operation for mid-December, 1970.

Mother telephoned after the surgery had been performed on December the 11th and told all of her children that it had been a great success, news which we expected. Daddy began recovering quickly.

A few days later I called his room and I was convinced that he was getting well when he exhibited his normal irritability. My mother answered the phone and told me that he was anxious to get out of the hospital and back to work. When I asked to speak to him, I could hear him in the background say: "I don't have time to talk to her." It was the kind of remark a healthy Mendel Rivers would have made. Unfortunately, those were the last words I ever heard my father say.

A few days before Christmas, Daddy experienced a severe fibrillation of the heart. Mother was in the room with him, as usual, when he suddenly slumped over in his bed. At her call for help, a team of doctors rushed into the room.

"Your father has suffered a slight setback," Mother calmly said when she called later that day.

My sister, brother and I arrived the next day. We were allowed to visit our father for brief times in the intensive care unit of the hospital. The first time I saw him, I was relieved that he recognized me or anybody else, for that matter. He had suffered more than a slight setback.

For the next several days, we were given encouragement about his condition. We shopped for Christmas presents, attended a Christmas Eve service in the Church of the Advent and somehow managed to remain relatively cheerful during a very long Christmas Day. I'm not sure exactly why, but it seemed especially significant to us then that Daddy lived through Christmas Day. But we all knew that his condition was not improving as all thought it would be doing.

In the early hours of December 28th, Dr. Kirklin called to tell us that my father had died. This "Rock of Gibraltar," this man who seemed totally indestructible, had lost his toughest battle—the one with his heart.

The plane bearing the body of Mendel Rivers dropped down through the wintry, overcast skies and prepared to land at the Charleston Air Force Base. Absolute silence fell among the small crowd of enlisted men and officers who watched. Airmen working on nearby C-141 Starlifter planes came to attention. The flag-draped casket was lowered from the plane and carried through a line formed by a 16-man honor guard.

President Nixon issued a statement in which he said: "Throughout his career, Congressman Rivers held unswervingly to the belief that the freedom that exists in the modern world is inextricably tied to the military strength of the United States. He fought for that belief in committee, in the Congress, in the country. No shifting national opinion, no amount of hostile criticism, deterred him from the course he deemed right for America. In his death, I have lost a friend upon whom I could rely in times of great difficulty; South Carolina has lost one of the most distinguished men in her history and America has lost a patriot."

Daddy's body lay in state at Grace Episcopal Church in Charleston for 24 hours prior to the funeral services. Eight thousand people came to the church in cold, wet weather to file by his open casket to pay their last respects. An honor guard made up of volunteers from all the military services stood by the highly-polished mahogany casket. A local newspaper account noted that among the mourners who walked past were "men in work clothes, bearded youths, elderly people, whites and blacks...A tall Negro man, wearing an American Legionnaire's cap stopped momentarily in front of the casket, stood at attention and briskly saluted."

A planeload of dignitaries from Washington came for the funeral services—Congressmen, diplomats, military officers and Secretary of

Defense Melvin Laird, sent as President Nixon's personal representative.

The weather had turned sunny, but was still quite cold. Friends of Mendel Rivers crowded into Grace Church, which was too small to accommodate the large crowds. The service was broadcast in two other churches, as well. I wondered, when I saw so many people standing in the back of the church and along the side aisles—about a block of empty pews near the front of the church. The seating had been intended for the use of the servicemen who had stood by my father's casket over the last day and night. My mother was disappointed to learn later that there had been a mix-up in communications and instructions, leaving the seats unfilled.

I remember feeling, through the numbness, immense pride as the funeral procession moved slowly out of the city. Everything seemed strangely quiet and still.

It was rather haunting the way the route from Charleston to the graveyard in St. Stephen summoned up the life and accomplishments of Mendel Rivers. All of us felt it.

We passed Rivers Avenue, which was uncannily close to so much that had been a part of my father's efforts; his boyhood home on O'Hear Avenue in North Charleston; the Navy Yard he had helped to develop into one of the most important in the country; the Charleston Air Force Base (with its Rivers Entrance Gate) which he had helped to gain status as a critical facility. It was one of his proud accomplishments that the brand-new Naval hospital had just been completed and was situated on Rivers Avenue across, coincidentally, from a bronze bust of him that had been erected years before. Further along in the ride we came close to the turn-off to Men-Riv Park, a military housing area, and to several defense-related plants which he had helped to bring to the Charleston area.

All along the way to the small town of St. Stephen for the interment, "his" people lined the streets and highway to watch the procession. They had stopped their cars on the highways and stood silently on the edge of the roads.

Except for one car. A small green sports car darted past the long line of cars heading for the cemetery just as we left the city limits of Charleston. It was such a surprise, so out-of-keeping with the solemnity that surrounded us, that I never really forgot it. Five years later I met a *News and Courier* newspaper photographer to whom I told the story when we had somehow gotten into a conversation about my father's funeral. *He* had been the driver of that lone, seemingly disrespectful, vehicle, and had been instructed by his editor to beat the funeral procession to St. Stephen in order to obtain pictures of its arrival.

We gathered outside the small church that my father, as a young boy, had attended.

A bugle played taps and a formation of Air Force Phantom Jets, with one plane symbolically absent, flew over the small graveyard. Then a lone C-5A, the world's largest airplane—for which Daddy had worked so hard—passed over the crowd of several hundred and tipped its wings. Secretary Laird presented my mother with the American flag that had draped the coffin of L. Mendel Rivers.

During the graveside services, my brother spoke for our family and our father's friends and admirers better than anyone else when he said:
> "L. Mendel Rivers has come to rest...
> A man of the people, his strength, it can
> be fairly said, did come from you. It was
> his people who made him everything he was. I
> hope you never forget it. He never did.
> Dynamism...love...courage...He had a
> great and wonderful heart, filled with beauty
> and love for people. He chose everything
> carefully—his ideas and values—and once
> chosen, he never wavered, deviated or detoured.
> He simply didn't know how.
> He died loved and mourned by millions and
> surrounded by his family. No man could ask for
> more."

INDEX